Dictionary of Theological Terms

in Simplified English

Debbie Dodd

A Simplified Dictionary of Theology

A Product

Submitted to the Faculty of

Western Conservative Baptist Seminary

Portland, Oregon

In Partial Fulfillment

of the Requirements for the Degree

Master of Theology

by

Debbie L. Dodd

This work was originally Debbie's thesis/product for her ThM in Theology at Western Seminary. It was written with the goal of making theology more accessible for laypeople in the US or international students around the world. Debbie was associate professor at Western for 3 years teaching Hebrew, Introduction to Biblical Languages and Theology. Since 1995, she and her husband, Peter, have been missionaries with WorldVenture in Taiwan. Debbie teaches Hebrew, Greek and Bible at Taiwan Conservative Baptist Seminary and is involved in leadership training and church planting. Her prayer is that as a result of this dictionary people will understand and grow more deeply in love with our great God and Savior!

DICTIONARY OF THEOLOGY

ABBA. (Aramaic word: abba, father.) A name for God in the New Testament. It is the name children used for their fathers. Therefore, it shows close family relationship and intimate respect. It is used by Jesus in Mk. 14:36. Also, Paul uses it in Rom. 8:15-16 and Gal. 4:6. (See also Adoption, Theology Proper.)

ABSOLUTION. (From Latin: absolvo, to set free.) To announce that sins* are forgiven.* In Roman Catholic* practice, a person must first be sorry for their sins (contrition), then confess* them to a priest.* Next, that person must do penance* (actions to pay for sins done). Then the priest announces that a person's sins are forgiven (absolution). (See also Confess, Confession; Forgiveness; Penance.)

ABSOLUTISM. A system of ethics* (rules for good and evil) which says there are rules or laws or truths which should never be broken. Those laws are always true in every place and time. (See also Ethics.)

ACCOMMODATION. Adapting a message to fit the hearers. In theology, it is the principle that God communicated the gospel* in a way we as humans could understand. There are two views regarding accommodation. (1) Some use it to interpret anthropomorphisms* (descriptions of God using human terms). (2) Others use it to interpret the words of Jesus. They claim Jesus said things which were not true just to agree with the Jewish beliefs of his day. (See also

Anthropo-morphism; Contextualization.)

ADAMIC SIN. (SEE ORIGINAL SIN.)

ADONAI. (Hebrew word: 'adonai, my lord.) Name for God meaning ruler over everything. It is used for either a human or divine master by a servant. (See also Sovereignty.)

ADOPTION. The part of salvation* in which God makes the sinner his child. It is a result of conversion.* That person now has the rights and responsibilities of being part of God's family. Only Paul uses the term (Rom. 8:15, 23; 9:4; Gal. 4:5; Eph. 1:5). (See also Abba; Heir; Inheritance.)

ADOPTIONISM. The view that Jesus was just a good man before becoming God. During his life (usually seen to be at his baptism), God "adopted" him to be his son. They believe man became God, not God became man. This view is not accepted by orthodox* Christians today. (See also Christology; Hypostatic Union.)

ADVENT. (From Latin: adventus, coming, arrival.) The coming of Jesus. (1) His first advent is when he was born of a virgin* as a Jew* in Bethlehem. (2) His second advent is the second coming,* when he returns at the end of the age.* (3) It is also a season during the church year. It is the four Sundays before Christmas in which believers celebrate his first coming. (See also Incarnation; Second Coming.)

ADVENTISM. (1) The belief that Jesus will return at any time. When he returns he will set up his 1000 year rule on earth (millennium*). (2) It is most often used for the Seventh day Adventists denomination. (See also Imminent; Millennium.)

ADVERSARY. Someone who is against you or who is your enemy. In the Bible it describes Satan. * He is the enemy of God and of God's people. (See also Satan.)

ADVOCATE. (SEE PARACLETE.)

AFTERLIFE. Life after death. It is the place or nature of a person after physical death. It may refer to heaven* or hell,* resurrection of the body,* life forever, etc. (See also Eschatology; Everlasting Life.)

AGE, AGES. A long period of time. In the Bible it is usually specified only by the context. In the NT there are two ages: "this age" and "the age to come." "This age" is the present time. Earth is its focus. Satan* is its ruler (2 Cor. 4:4; Gal. 1:4). "The age to come" is the time of peace and righteousness* promised by the OT. It the time of the Messiah.* It will be fulfilled completely in the future time after Jesus returns. He will be the ruler and it will be the time of eternal life* (Mk. 10:30). But he has broken into this present age in the resurrection* of Jesus and in the coming of the Holy Spirit.* It is also called "the end of the age" (Matt. 24:3). (See also Eschatology; Inaugurated Eschatology.)

AGNOSTICISM. (From Greek: agnosis, unknown.) The

belief that we cannot know God. An agnostic believes two things. (1) We cannot know if there is a God or not. (2) If there is a God, we cannot know him. (See also Atheism; Theism.)

ALIENATION. Being separate from God. Sin* has destroyed the relationship with God. All humans are born alienated from God because we are born as a part of Adam's family. (See also Original Sin.)

ALLEGORICAL INTERPRETATION, ALLEGORIZING. (From Greek: allegoria, describing something in the image of another.) A way of interpreting the Bible. It looks for a hidden, symbolic* meaning instead of the plain, ordinary sense that the whole context requires (literalism*). It then says the hidden meaning is the true meaning and gives authority to it. Allegorical interpretation was used mostly in the Middle Ages. It is rejected by most Bible interpreters today. This is different from the allegorical* form of speech found in the Bible. This form of speech is specifically stated (Gal. 4:21ff) or clear by the context (Prov. 5:15ff). (See also Allegory; Hermeneutics; Literalism.)

ALLEGORY. (From Greek: allegoria, describing something in the image of another.) A form of speech which uses a picture to express an abstract truth. It is longer and has more detail than a metaphor. It is used as an illustration like in Gal. 4. Daniel and Revelation are other examples which use allegory. This is specifically stated (Gal. 4:21ff) or clear by the context (Prov. 5:15ff). In this way, it is different from the allegorical* method of interpreting the Bible. (See also Allegorical Interpretation, Allegorizing; Analogy.)

ALPHA AND OMEGA. The names of the first and last letters in the Greek alphabet. It is used as a title for God and Christ (Rev. 1:8; 21:6; 22:13). The phrase means "the beginning and the end." It shows God's eternity.* He began everything and will bring it all to an end. (See also Eternity.)

AMILLENNIALISM. (From Latin: a-, not, mille, thousand, and annus, year.) The belief that the rule of Christ is happening now. It is not a future event. That rule is spiritual, not visible. The 1000 years in Rev. 20:4-6 is understood as the period of time between the cross and the end of the age.* (See also Millennium; Premillennialism; Postmillennialism.)

ANALOGY. (From Greek: analogia, proportion, correspondence.) A way of describing something by the use of something that is similar. The two are like each other in some ways, but different in other ways. An unknown object or idea is described by something like it that is known. Something in creation* is often used as an analogy to describe God. For example, when Ps. 18:2 says "My God is my Rock" it does not mean that God is stone. It is an analogy to show that he is a place of safety and protection. (See also Anthropomorphism; Hermeneutics.)

ANALOGY OF FAITH, ANALOGIA FIDEI. The belief that the Bible is a unified whole in what it teaches. It does not contradict itself. So what the Bible teaches in one place must agree with what it teaches in other places. Therefore, we can use the rest of the Bible and theology* to evaluate a theological statement. This is based on a high view of the authority* and inspiration* of the Bible. Out of this belief comes a principle of interpreting the Bible. It says that the clearer parts of the Bible guide our interpretation of the less clear parts. Sometimes a distinction is made between "Analogy of Faith" (creedal* statements) and "Analogy of Scripture" (theological* statements). (See also Hermeneutics; Creed.)

ANALOGY OF SCRIPTURE. (SEE ANALOGY OF FAITH, ANALOGIA FIDEI.)

ANGEL. (From Greek: angelos, messenger.) A heavenly being created by God. They do the work of God, worship* and serve Him. They also minister* to believers. Cherubim and seraphim are names for different types of angels. (See also Angelology; Demons, Demon Possession.)

ANGELOLOGY. (From Greek: angelos, messenger, and logos, word.) The part of theology that deals with spiritual beings. It is the teaching about angels,* demons,* and Satan.* It includes both who they are and what they do. (See also Angel; Demons, Demon Possession; Satan.)

ANIMISM. (From Latin: animus, breath, soul.) One of the major religions of the world. It is the belief that all physical objects (i.e., stones, trees, etc.) have living spirits in them. Therefore, they must be worshipped.* It is a part of many non-Christian religions. It is also called "primitive religions." (See also Polytheism; Spiritism.)

ANNIHILATIONISM. (From Latin: nihil, nothing.) The belief that some people will stop existing after death. It usually means hell* will only be for a short time or not at all. It comes from the view that being able to live forever is a gift that God only gives to some people (conditional immortality*). Annihilationism is not taught in the Bible. (See also Conditional Immortality; Hell; Immortality.)

ANOINT. The act of putting oil on a person or thing. This sets apart that person or thing for God. It is done to give a special job, blessing or power. Kings were anointed in Bible days. Messiah,* one of the titles for Jesus, literally means "The Anointed One." The Roman Catholic* Church also has a sacrament* of anointing called "unction." (See also Consecrate.)

ANTHROPOCENTRIC. (From Greek: anthropos, human, and kentrikos, center.) The belief or practice that humans are the center of everything, not God. Humans and their needs and values are most important. (See also Theocentric.)

ANTHROPOLOGICAL ARGUMENTS. (From Greek: anthropos, human.) The attempt to prove there is a God based on what humans are like. A common form of this is the moral argument.* (See also Theistic Proofs; Moral Argument.)

ANTHROPOLOGY. (From Greek: anthropos, human,

and logos, word.) (1) In theology, it is the part of the theological system that deals with humanity. It describes their origins, nature and destiny. (2) It is also the academic study of people and their ways. The subject is the physical nature of people and their ways of living. (See also Man.)

ANTHROPOMORPHISM. (From Greek: anthropos, human, and morphe, form.) Describing God in human ways. It attributes human qualities, actions or feelings to God. It is looking at God from a human perspective. For example, the arm of God in Jer. 32:17 does not mean a physical arm, but is used to show his power. (See also Accommodation.)

ANTI-SEMITISM. The hatred of Jewish people.

ANTICHRIST. (From Greek: anti, against, and Christos, Christ.) (1) The person who is the great enemy of Christ. He will come in the last days* saying he is the Christ. Only I Jn. 2:18, 22; 4:3 speaks of him by name. (2) However, the NT often speaks of enemies of Christ. Throughout history, some have called certain people or offices (i.e., leaders, govern-ments, churches, etc.) the Antichrist. (See also Eschatology.)

ANTILEGOMENA. (From Greek: anti, against, and legein, to say; literally: to disagree.) A term used for the NT books which were not universally accepted as part of the Bible. Some sections of the church said they should be accepted. Others said they should not. They included James, 2 Peter, 2 & 3 John, and Jude. These were not the books that everyone agreed should be in the Bible (homologoumena*). These were also not the books that everyone agreed should not be in the Bible. (See also Canon; Homologoumena.)

ANTINOMIANISM. (From Greek: anti, against, and nomos, law.) The view that the believer should not follow the moral laws of the OT. This is because we are saved by grace.* It says grace excuses us from the need for discipline or holy living. If we follow the law then we reject grace. It is grace which both saves* and sanctifies* us. It is based heavily on Galatians. (See also Grace; Law; Legalism.)

ANTINOMY. (From Greek: anti, against, and nomos, law.) Two or more true statements that seem to contradict each other. But, if we understood things like God does, they would not contradict each other. An example is that Jesus is both God and man. (See also Paradox.)

ANTITYPE. (SEE TYPE.)

APOCALYPTIC, APOCALYPSE. (Greek word: apokalypsis, to remove a covering from.) (1) A type of book which reveals or shows us something about spiritual mysteries.* They include visions of prophecies* and many symbols.* They speak of judgment* and the end of the age.* Daniel and Revelation are the main books of this type in the Bible. There are also other smaller parts of books (i.e., Isa. 13; 65-66). (2) It is also used to describe the coming of the Day of the Lord.* It will come suddenly and destroy all evil. It will come from outside this world.

(3) The book of Revelation is also called The Apocalypse. (See also Eschatology.)

APOCRYPHA. (From Greek: apokrypha, the hidden things.) (From Greek: apokrypha, the hidden things.) A group of books which were not included in the Protestant* or Eastern Orthodox* Bibles. These churches decided they were not inspired* by God. The books of the OT Apocrypha were written in the time between the OT and NT. These books are included in the Roman Catholic* Bible. The books of the NT Apocrypha were written after the first century after Christ. They are not included in any Bible. (See also Canon; Inspiration, Bible.)

APOLLINARIANISM. A view of Christ started by Apollinarius (c. 361-390), Bishop of Laodicea. It teaches that Christ was fully God, but not fully human. He only took on a human body and soul,* not a human spirit.* The divine* spirit replaced the human spirit. This view is not accepted by orthodox* Christians today. (See also Christology; Deity of Christ; Hypostatic Union.)

APOLOGETICS. (From Greek: apologia, to defend, give an answer.) The intelligent defense of the Christian faith. It answers honest questions about the truthfulness of the gospel.* Its tasks are to (1) defend the gospel against attacks or errors and (2) give reasons for its truth. (I Pet. 3:15.) (See also Systematic Theology.)

APOSTASY. (From Greek: apo, away, and stasis, standing.) Choosing to turn away from Christ after believing* in him. It can be a definite choice to reject

Christ. Or it can be a result of a continual lack of interest in Christ. Judas Iscariot is a NT example of an apostate. It is different from backsliding* because the unbelief is permanent, not just for a short time. It is also different from heresy* because apostates do not call themselves Christians anymore. (See also Backsliding; Heresy.)

APOSTLE. (From Greek: apo, from, and stellein, to send.) A person called and sent out for a certain purpose with the authority of the one who sent them. (1) In the NT, it is most often used for the twelve men Jesus chose as his special disciples.* (2) Also, Paul and a few other people are called apostles. (3) Jesus is also called "the Apostle" (Heb. 3:1). (4) Roman Catholics* use it for their missionaries.* Some Protestants* believe today the spiritual gift* of apostles (1 Cor. 12:28) is given to missionaries. (See also Disciple.)

APOSTOLIC SUCCESSION. The belief that the authority* of a church has been passed on from person to person from the apostles* to leaders today. These leaders then pass it on to others that they choose. It is taught in Roman Catholic* and some other churches with an Episcopal* church government.* (See also Church Government.)

ARIANISM. A view of Christ started by Arius (c. 250-336), a North African priest. It teaches that Jesus is not fully God. There can only be one God. So they say Jesus was created by God out of nothing and is very special. He is the first and greatest creature. He is like God, but he is not God. Today, Jehovah's Witnesses teach

this view. This view is not accepted by orthodox*
Christians today. (See also Christology; Deity of Christ;
Hypostatic Union.)

ARK OF THE COVENANT. The wooden box that was
placed inside the Holy of Holies* in the temple. It was
about 4 x 2 1/2 x 2 1/2 feet (120 x 76 x 76 cm) and
covered with gold. The lid was called the mercy seat.*
Inside were the two tablets of the ten commandments, a
pot of manna (the food God gave during the Exodus), and
Aaron's rod (Exod. 25:10-22). It was the place where God
met with the high priest once a year (Lev. 16). It is also
called the Ark of Testimony or the Ark of the Lord. (See
also Decalogue; Holy of Holies; Mercy Seat; Temple; Will
of God.)

ARMAGEDDON. (Greek word: harmagedon, name of a
place, Armaged-don.) A place spoken of in Rev. 16:16.
The armies of God and Satan* will fight the final battle at
the end of the ages* there. There are many questions
about where it is. However, most scholars think it refers
to the mountain of Megiddo, about 50 miles (80km) north
of Jerusalem. (See also Eschatology.)

ARMINIANISM. The system of theology* started by
Jacob Arminius (1560-1609), a Dutch theologian. Human
freedom* is its focus. It has five main points. (1) God
saves those sinners he knows ahead of time will believe.
(2) Christ died for all people, not just the elect.* (3) A
person needs God's grace* to believe. (4) All humans can
freely respond to or resist God's grace. (5) Christians can
lose their salvation* if they stop believing. These are in

response to Calvinistic* theology. (See also Atonement, Unlimited; Calvinism; Foreknowledge; Freedom, Free Will, Freedom of the Will; Wesleyan.)

ASCENSION, THE. (From Latin: ascendere, to go up.) The time when Jesus went up bodily from earth into heaven.* It happened forty days after his resurrection* (Lk. 24:51; Acts 1:9). (See also Resurrection of Christ.)

ASCETICISM. (From Greek: askein, to work, train the body, exercise.) The method of trying to be holy* by discipline and giving up the things of the world.* The three marks are usually poverty, chastity (living without the pleasures of this world), and obedience* to God. (See also Holy, Holiness.)

ASEITY. (From Latin: a , from, and se , oneself.) To have life within oneself. God has life in himself. He does not need anyone else so that he can live. Jn. 5:26 and Acts 17:23 25 teach this. In contrast, we need God so we can live (Acts 17:28). God is the only one who has aseity. (See also Attributes of God; Necessary Being.)

ASSURANCE (OF SALVATION). The sure knowledge God gives a believer that they are saved. The believers know they are children of God and that their sins* are forgiven.* The sure knowledge is based on 1 Jn. 5:11-13. (See also Eternal Security; Perseverance.)

ATHEISM. (From Greek: a-, without, and theos, God.) The belief that there is no God. Practical atheism means living life without God. (See also Agnosticism; Theism;

Secularism.)

ATONEMENT. Bringing God and believers back into a good relationship. Sin* broke the relationship with God. In the OT, atonement was made by performing sacrifices. In the NT, Christ's death on the cross* took away the barriers so there could be a relationship again. There are many different theories about how that could happen. (See also Expiation; Justification, Justify; Propitiation; Reconciliation; Redemption.)

ATONEMENT, DEFINITE. (SEE ATONEMENT, LIMITED.)

ATONEMENT, EXTENT OF THE. The question of whom Christ die to save.* Some say it was only for the elect, those chosen by God (limited*). Others say it was for all people (unlimited*). (See also Atonement, Limited; Atonement, Unlimited.)

ATONEMENT, GOVERNMENTAL THEORY. The view that says the purpose of Christ's death was to satisfy God's justice.* It says God is like a ruler and has to uphold his moral law.* When we sin* we break it. God wants very much to forgive* people. So Christ died to show us how bad sin is and how important it is to follow God's law. It is often a part of Wesleyan* theology. It was started by Hugo Grotius (1583-1645) of Holland. (See also Just, Justice.)

ATONEMENT, LIMITED. The belief that Christ died for only the elect,* those chosen by God. It is often called definite atonement. It is part of Calvinism* and is the "L" in TULIP.* (See also Atonement, Unlimited; TULIP.)

ATONEMENT, MORAL INFLUENCE THEORY.
The view that the purpose of Christ's death was to show us how much God loves us. That should make us love others. Abelard (1079-1142) of Brittany, started this view. (See also Socinianism.)

ATONEMENT, PENAL SUBSTITUTION THEORY.
The view that Christ died to take the penalty of sin.* The judgment for sin is death. Christ paid it for us. He was our sacrifice.* (See also Substitute.)

ATONEMENT, RANSOM THEORY. The view that Christ's death was a payment to Satan.* Sinful humans belong to Satan. Therefore, he has a right to demand a price to free them. Christ took their place so that they could be freed from Satan's control. (See also Ransom.)

ATONEMENT, SATISFACTION THEORY. The view of Christ's death started by Anselm (1033-1109) of Canterbury. Humans robbed God by sinning.* We broke God's honor. So Christ became a man so he could take our place. He was also God so he could pay a big enough price. His death paid God what we owed him and gave him back his honor. (See also Satisfaction.)

ATONEMENT, SUBSTITUTION THEORY. The view that Christ died in our place. We should have died, but he died instead of us. It is usually a part of the penal* view. (See also Atonement, Penal Substitution Theory;

Substitution.)

ATONEMENT, UNIVERSAL. (SEE ATONEMENT, UNLIMITED.)

ATONEMENT, UNLIMITED. The belief that Christ died for all people, not just the elect.* However, this does not necessarily mean that all people will be saved.* People must believe* to be saved. (See also Atonement, Limited.)

ATONEMENT, VICARIOUS. The view that Christ's death was on behalf of sinners. We got the benefits. He did something for us. It is often contrasted with substitution* where Christ took the exact penalty of our sin.* (See also Atonement, Substitution Theory.)

ATTRIBUTES OF GOD. The qualities or characteristics of God. They describe God.* They are a part of who God is, not just added to Him. Without them he would not be God. Examples are love,* mercy* and eternity.* (See also Essence; Theology Proper.)

AUGUSTINIANISM. The system of theology* and philosophy of Augus-tine (354-430), Bishop* of Hippo. A main point is that humans are not able to do anything to save* themselves. Therefore, God chose certain people to be saved before the world began (predestination*). Another main point is that faith* is more important that reason. In many ways it is a combination of the philosophy of Plato and Christian theology. Calvinism* is a kind of Augustinianism. (See also Total Inability;

Predestination.)

AUTHORITY. The right to command action or belief.*
(1) It is used in many ways in the Bible: to forgive* sin
(Lk. 5:24); to make demons* leave a person (Mk. 6:7); for
government leaders (Rom. 13:1), etc. God is the highest
authority. (2) In theology, it is used of both the Bible* and
the church.* (See also Bible; Church; Tradition.)

BACKSLIDING. Falling into sin* or unbelief* for a
short time after one has been saved.* It is shorter or a less
serious turning away than apostasy.* (See also Apostasy;
Heresy.)

BAPTISM. (From Greek: baptizo, to wash or dip.) The
act of applying water to show that a person has become a
part of the family of God. It shows they have been united
with Christ.* They have died with Christ (shown by going
under the water) and have been given new life in Him
(shown by coming out of the water). There are many
disagreements about baptism. Who should be baptized
(infants or just believers)? Who should do the baptizing?
How should baptism be done (immer-sion,* sprinkling,*
pouring*)? What exactly does it mean? What exactly
happens at baptism? (See also Ordinance; Sacrament;
Baptism, Believer; Baptism, Infant; Immersion; Pouring;
Sprinkling.)

BAPTISM, BELIEVER. The belief that only those who
have personal faith in Christ should be baptized.* The
main argument is that baptism is a picture of being united
with Christ.* A different view is infant baptism.* (See

also Baptism, Infant.)

BAPTISM IN/OF/WITH THE HOLY SPIRIT. When the Holy Spirit* lives in and gives power to a believer. In the Bible, John the Baptist promised Jesus would bring this blessing* (Matt. 3:11 12). At Pentecost* this promise was fulfilled (Acts 2). In theology* today there is disagreement about what it is and when it happens. Pentecostals* and some Wesleyans* teach that it happens sometime after conversion.* They say it is a "second blessing"* which is intended for all believers, but only some receive it. Others teach that it happens at conversion and all believers have it (1 Cor. 12:13). They say it makes people a part of the Body of Christ.* Most people agree that it is different from the filling of the Holy Spirit.* (See also Body of Christ; Filled with the Spirit; Second Blessing.)

BAPTISM, INFANT. The belief that the children of Christians should be baptized.* The main argument is that baptism is the NT form of OT circumcision* which brings the child into a covenant* relationship with God. It is also called "paedobaptism." A different view is believer's baptism.* (See also Baptism, Believer; Covenant Theology.)

BAPTISMAL REGENERATION. The belief that when a person is bap-tized* they are regenerated,* made spiritually alive in Christ. Jn. 3:3 and Tit. 3:5 are usually used as the basis. It is sometimes found in Roman Catholic* and Church of Christ theologies. This view often teaches the act of baptism has the power actually to save* a person. (See also Baptism.)

BELIEF. (SEE FAITH.)

BEMA SEAT. (SEE JUDGMENT SEAT.)

BENEVOLENCE. The concern for the good of other people. It is God's unselfish interest for his people for their benefit. Deut. 7:7 8 and Jn. 15:9 17 teach this truth. Benevolence is a part of his love.* (See also Love; Attributes of God.)

BIBLE. (From Greek: biblion, book.) The books included in the OT and NT. It is God's revelation* of himself to humans. "Scripture" is another name used for it which means "writings." (See also Canon; Hermeneutics.)

BIBLICAL CRITICISM. (SEE CRITICISM, BIBLICAL.)

BIBLICAL THEOLOGY. This term is used in two main ways. (1) It is a way of doing theology* which focuses on a passage of the Bible in its own context. It is looking at the Bible in its own terms, questions, issues and thought forms. Its main focus is on the meaning of the Bible for its own day. For example, when studying Gen. 3 it would look at it in the context of Genesis and its message for that day. It would not study it with other passages teaching about sin* (as systematic theology* would). (2) It is also a movement that was strong between about 1945 and 1965 in North America and Europe. It was connected with neo orthodoxy* and used methods of "higher criticism."* It says revelation* is focused on the acts of God in history. This is opposed to Liberal Theology* which says revelation is God at work in humans. It is also opposed to Fundamentalism* which says revelation is in the Bible. (3) Any theology which is based on and faithful to the teachings of the Bible is called "Biblical Theology." (See also Systematic Theolo-gy; Neo Orthodoxy; Heilsgeschichte; Criticism, Higher.)

BIBLIOLOGY. (From Greek: biblion, book, and logos, word.) The part of theology that deals with the Bible.* It includes topics like revelation,* authority* and inspiration* of Scripture. (See also Authority; Bible; Inspiration, Bible; Revelation.)

BISHOP. In Greek this title meant "overseer." (1) In the NT it was a person who was given leadership over a church.* Often in the NT it seems to be another name for elder.* (2) Today in the Episcopal* form of church government,* it is the person who is leader over many churches in a certain area. (See also Episcopal Government; Elder.)

BLASPHEMY. (From Greek: blasphemein, to speak evil of.) To say bad or false things against or to insult another person or thing. It means to curse or act against something sacred or special. It is used especially of taking away the honor of God. Blasphemy against the Holy Spirit is the "unpardonable sin"* (Matt. 12:31). (See also Unpardonable Sin.)

BLESS. A very common word in the Bible. When

humans bless, it means to praise or thank God. When God blesses, it means giving something good to humans. (See also Praise.)

BLOOD. (1) In the Bible, it often refers to life. (2) It also refers to the blood of Christ. There is disagreement over what that means. Most say it refers to his death. Some say it refers to his life that was poured out. All agree that it is used with the idea of sacrifice.* (See also Cross; Sacrifice.)

BODY OF CHRIST. (1) Literally, Jesus' physical body. (2) More often it is a word picture the NT uses to describe the church.* Jesus is its head (Eph. 1:22-23). All believers together make up the body. It shows the fact that the church is one, yet each member has different gifts.* The church is blessed* by all the different gifts. Therefore we must encourage them. All are to work together for the same goals. It also shows that the church is to carry out Christ's saving plan in ways the world can see. It is the focus of 1 Cor. 12:12 31. (See also Church; Spiritual Gifts.)

BORN AGAIN. A phrase Jesus used with Nicodemus to refer to a spiritual birth (Jn. 3:3). It is another term for regeneration.* It is when the Holy Spirit gives a person new spiritual life. (See also Regeneration.)

BRIDE, BRIDEGROOM. A word picture the NT uses to describe the church.* Christ is the bridegroom and the church is the bride. It shows that Christ loves the church. It also shows that the church is to respond in love and obedience.* In Jewish culture, a bridegroom came to get his bride. Just like that, Christ will return to be joined to the church (Rev. 19:7; 21:2, 9). (See also Church.)

CALL. (1) God's invitation to humans to receive his grace* in a special way. It is used of those who are called to salvation* (Mk. 2:17). (2) It is also used for those who are called to serve God in a special way (Rom. 1:1). (See also Calling, Effectual; Election; Predestination.)

CALVINISM. The system of theology* started by John Calvin (1509-64) of France. God's rule or sovereignty* is its focus. It has five points. (1) Sin* affects every part of a person. (2) God elects* or chooses to save people according to his choice alone, not because of anything they do. (3) Christ died for only certain people, the elect,* not all people. (4) God's saving grace* always works and humans cannot resist it. (5) God will keep true Christians faithful to the end. These are in contrast to Arminian* theology. It is a type of Reformed theology.* (See also Arminianism; Atonement, Limited; Elect; Election; Irresistible Grace; Perseverance; Sovereignty; Total Depravity; Wesleyan.)

CANON. (From Greek: kanon, a measuring rod.) (1) The group of books that the early church decided were authoritative* because they were inspired* by God. They are the 66 books of the Bible for Protestants.* Roman Catholics* have 80 books which includes the Apocrypha.* (2) "Canon" is also the name of a church officer.* This person is responsible for taking care of large church buildings (cathedrals). (See also Authority; Inspiration,

Bible; Offices, Church.)

CANONIZATION. (From Greek: kanon, a measuring rod.) (1) The Roman Catholic process of declaring a person to be a saint.* (2) It also is used for the process of deciding which books were a part of the Bible.* (See also Saint; Canon.)

CARNAL. (SEE FLESH, FLESHLY.)

CATECHISM. (From Greek: katecheo, to teach.) A statement or book that teaches the basic truths of Christianity. It is usually used with children or new believers. It often should be memorized. (See also Creed.)

CATHOLIC. (From Greek: katholikos, throughout the whole, general.) Universal or general. (1) Most often it means the Roman Catholic* Church as distinct from Protestant* churches. (2) It also means the universal church,* all believers in all times. (3) It also refers to the "catholic" or general epistles* of the NT. They were written to churches in general and not just one church. Those include James, 1 & 2 Peter, 1, 2, & 3 John and Jude. "Catholic" is always capitalized in the first meaning, but not in the other two. (See also Catholicism, Roman; Church, Universal.)

CATHOLICISM, ROMAN. The churches* which accept the bishop of Rome as Pope.* It is distinct from Protestant* and Eastern Orthodox* churches in several ways. They include: (1) The Catholic Church stands between humans and God as a mediator.* (2) The Pope is the earthly leader and highest human authority* in the church. (3) The sacra-ments* give grace to those who participate. (4) The Bible* and the tradition* of the church have equal authority as God's revelation.* (See also Orthodox Church; Pope; Protestantism.)

CHARISMATA. (SEE GIFTS.)

CHARISMATIC MOVEMENT. (From Greek: charismata, gifts of grace.) A term used to describe a movement in the church that began in the 1960's. It emphasizes the use of all the spiritual gifts,* especially the miraculous* ones. A very important gift is speaking in tongues* (using a language that the speaker does not know) as a prayer language. It also teaches that the baptism with the Holy Spirit* is a giving of special power and comes after conversion.* Charismatics usually try to renew and reform mainline churches. In this way it is different from Pente-costalism* who form new churches. An older name for charismatics is Neo-Pentecostalism. (See also Pentecostalism; Tongues, Speaking In; Baptism In/With/Of The Holy Spirit.)

CHERUBIM. (SEE ANGEL.)

CHILIASM. (SEE MILLENNIUM.)

CHOOSE, CHOSEN. (SEE ELECTION.)

CHRIST. (From Greek: chrio, to anoint.) The title for Jesus meaning "The Anointed One."* It is the Greek word for the Hebrew, "Messiah."* (See also Anoint; Messiah; Jesus.)

CHRIST OF FAITH. (SEE HISTORICAL JESUS.)

CHRIST, WORK OF. (SEE WORK OF CHRIST.)

CHRISTLIKENESS. (SEE IMITATION OF CHRIST.)

CHRISTOLOGY. (From Greek: christos, Christ, and logos, word.) The part of theology* that deals with the person and work of Christ. (See also Christ; Work of Christ.)

CHURCH. (1) A building in which a local church* meets. (2) A denomination* (group of local churches). (3) The group of believers in Jesus Christ. It is the family of God. The church practices water baptism* as an identification with Christ. They also celebrate the Lord's Supper.* Jesus is the leader, the head. It has three main purposes: worship;* evangelism* (telling others about Jesus); and edification* (helping believers to grow in faith). It is based on the teachings of the apostles* and prophets.* (See also Church, Local; Church, Universal.)

CHURCH AND STATE. The relationship between the authority of the church and of the civil government. It often refers to the idea that the two are to be separate. (See also Civil Disobedience.)

CHURCH DISCIPLINE. (SEE DISCIPLINE, CHURCH.)

CHURCH GOVERNMENT. The way churches are organized. There are three main types of church government (Congregationalism,* Episcopal,* and Presbyterian*.) The basic differences are who is given authority.* It is also called church polity. (See also Congregationalism; Episcopal Government; and Presbyterian Government.)

CHURCH, INVISIBLE. All people who are spiritually united to Christ.* It is called invisible because no one can see the hearts of other people. The term was first used by Augustine (354-430), Bishop of Hippo. Some people do not like to use the term because the church should not be invisible. It includes the same people as the universal church.* (See also Church, Local; Church, Visible; Church, Universal.)

CHURCH, LOCAL. A group of believers who gather together regularly in a certain place. They are organized. They use their spiritual gifts* to minister* both inside and outside the church. The contrast is the universal church* which is all true believers throughout history and in all places. (See also Church, Universal; Church, Invisible; Church, Visible.)

CHURCH, VISIBLE. All who are a part of the organized church* on earth today. They may or may not be saved.* It does not include believers who are not a part of a church or people who are not alive today. (See also Church, Invisible; Church, Local; Church, Universal.)

CHURCH, UNIVERSAL. All true believers throughout

history and in all places. Some say it includes believers from Pentecost* until Jesus returns. Others say it includes the people of God at all times. There is only one universal church.* Jesus is its leader. The NT calls it the "body of Christ."* It is sometimes called "catholic"* which means universal. The contrast is the local church* which is the group of believers who gather in a specific place. (See also Church, Local; Church, Invisible; Church, Visible.)

CIRCUMCISION. (From Latin: circum, around, and caedere, to cut.) The act of cutting off the foreskin of the male. In the OT it was the sign of God's promise* to Israel which began with Abraham (Gen. 17:11). It was the mark that said these people belong to God. In the NT, believers are told to "circumcise" the heart (Col. 2:11). That means being honestly sorry for sin* and showing that you belong to God. (See also Judaism.)

CIVIL DISOBEDIENCE. An action that is opposite of what the government laws command. People disobey because they believe the law is wrong or unjust. There is discussion in theology about if God allows it. On one side, Rom. 13 and 1 Pet. 2 say to obey the government because God uses it for good. On the other side, Daniel (Dan. 6), Peter (Acts 5), and Paul (Acts 16) disobeyed their government's laws. (See also Church and State.)

CIVIL RELIGION. The belief in a religion by a people that is in some way connected with their government. It is usually a part of their history. It also can be a religion based on culture.* (See also Church and State.)

CLEAN, UNCLEAN. Clean means ritually or ceremonially pure. In the OT, people, places and things could be made unclean or impure in many different ways. Certain foods, sicknesses and death could make someone or something unclean. It needed to be cleansed by something like sacrifice, water, blood, or fire. (See also Purify, Purification.)

CLEANSING. (SEE PURIFY, PURIFICATION.)

CLERGY. Those who have been set apart or ordained* for a specific ministry.* They are usually paid for their ministry. They also usually have some authority.* Believers who are not ordained are called "laity."* (See also Laity; Ordain, Ordination.)

COMFORTER, THE. (SEE PARACLETE.)

COMMON GRACE. The goodness God gives to all people. It includes things like God giving rain and sunshine to everyone (Matt. 5:45). Other examples are helping non-Christians to do good things and to limit sin.* In Wesleyanism* it may be the same as prevenient grace,* that grace given to all people so they can choose to believe.* (See also Efficacious Grace; Prevenient Grace; Irresistible Grace.)

COMMUNICATION OF ATTRIBUTES, COMMUNICATIA IDIOMATUM. A term used to describe the relationship between the human and divine* natures of Christ. It says that he was only one person.* So whatever is true of (attributed) either Christ's human or divine nature is true of his whole person. There is disagreement between Lutherans* and Calvinists* on how this happens. (See also Hypostatic Union.)

COMMUNION. (SEE LORD'S SUPPER.)

COMPARATIVE RELIGION. The study of many different religions to find how they are alike and different. It often is based on a belief that there is something in common with all religions. That which is in common is the true religion.

CONCURSUS. A term used to speak of the relationship between God's actions and the free* actions of his creation. The creatures (usually humans) are free to do what they wish. Yet, he uses their free actions to carry out his purposes. It is part of providence,* his care for his creation.* (See also Providence; Government, Divine.)

CONDEMN, CONDEMNATION. To find a person guilty* of wrong and punish them. It is God's judgment* against sin.* (See also Guilt; Judgment.)

CONDITIONAL IMMORTALITY. The teaching that the ability to live forever is a gift given by God only to believers. It is a type of annihilationism* (the belief that some people will not live after death) because the wicked will not live after death. It is not believed by most Christians. (See also Immortality; Annihilationism.)

CONFESS, CONFESSION. To say or agree with what is true. It is used in two different ways. (1) It means to tell God about your sins.* It is to agree with God about the evil of sin. (2) It also means to tell others about your faith* in Christ. (See also Witness, Testimony.)

CONGREGATIONALISM. A way that some churches are organized. Authority* is given to the church as a whole. Its model is that Christ is head and that all believers are priests.* Each church is independent and can govern or rule itself. (See also Church Government; Episcopal Government; Presbyterian Government; Priesthood of All Believers.)

CONSCIENCE. (From Latin: conscientia, to know together.) The ability to understand the difference between right and wrong. It is the sense that what I am doing is either good or bad. In the Bible it is the urge to do the good and not do the bad. It is something all persons are born with. (See also Ethics; Morality.)

CONSECRATE. To set apart someone or something so it can serve God in a special way. Either God, the person being consecrated, or another person may do the consecrating. (See also Anoint.)

CONSERVATION. (SEE PRESERVATION.)

CONSUBSTANTIATION. (SEE REAL PRESENCE.)

CONTEXTUALIZATION. Preparing an expression of the gospel* and theology in words and concepts understandable to the people hearing it today. It is not changing it, but making it understood. It is shaping the way theology* is explained to a specific culture.* Things like starting place and emphasis in theology is determined by contextualization. There are two different aspects. (1) Regarding time, we must contextualize the Bible from the first century culture of the Bible to the twentieth century. This is biblical interpretation (hermeneutics*). (2) Regarding cultures, we must contextualize theology from one culture of today to another. This is missions.* (See also Hermeneutics; Mission, Missions, Missiology.)

CONTINGENT BEING. (SEE NECESSARY BEING.)

CONVERSION. The human action of turning to Jesus. It includes both turning away from sin (repentance*) and turning to Jesus (faith*). It is the human response to the good news of God's salvation.* We only do it once as opposed to confession* which should be done as often as we sin. (See also Repentance; Faith; Salvation.)

CONVICT. Helping a person realize they have done something wrong. The NT says all three members of the Trinity* convict of sin.* However, it is mainly the job of the Holy Spirit* (Jn. 16:7 11). Also, God can use other people to convict of sin (2 Sam. 12). A person can respond either by being sorry and wanting to change (repentance*) or by rejecting the conviction. (See also Confession; Sin.)

COSMOLOGICAL ARGUMENT. (From Greek: kosmos, world.) The at-tempt to prove there is a God by what the world is like. There must be a God because someone must have created* the world. There must have been a cause. (See also Theistic Proofs; Creation; Cosmology.)

COSMOLOGY. (From Greek: kosmos, world and logos, word.) The study of the world, what it is like and how it began. It is often used as one of the ways to prove there is a God. (See also Cosmological Argument; Theistic Proofs.)

COVENANT. (1) The divine covenant is God's solemn promise* to enter into relationship with his people and bless them. God begins the relationship. He calls chosen humans into a lasting fellowship with him. He commits himself in love and grace* to his people who do not deserve it. They are to respond in thankful, loving obedience.* If they do not, there will be judgment.* However, that will not end their relationship. (2) In a broader sense a covenant is an agreement between two people or groups. Both promise to enter into relationship with and to do something for each other. (See also Covenant Theology.)

COVENANT OF GRACE. One of the three parts of Covenant Theology.* This is the promise* God made to the people he has chosen. God promises to save chosen sinners because of Christ's work. In response, the saved people promise to live in faith* and obedience* in relationship with God. (See also Covenant Theology; Covenant of Redemption; Covenant of Works.)

COVENANT OF REDEMPTION. One of the three parts of Covenant Theology.* It is the agreement between the Father and the Son before the world began. The Father appointed the Son to be Savior.* The Son agreed to be Savior and to represent the people God has chosen. (See also Covenant Theology; Covenant of Grace; Covenant of Works.)

COVENANT OF WORKS. One of the three parts of Covenant Theology.* This is the agreement God made with Adam. If Adam would obey God completely for a certain amount of time, God would give him life forever. If he did not obey, he would die. The results of his decision, death or life, would be passed on to all humans whom he represents. (See also Covenant Theology; Covenant of Grace; Covenant of Redemption; Original Sin.)

COVENANT THEOLOGY. A kind of Reformed Theology.* It sees the relationship between God and humans to be based on God's promise (covenant*). When Adam and Eve broke the covenant of works,* God graciously ended it and replaced it with the covenant of grace.* It emphasizes the free and sovereign* grace* of God who promises to bless his people only because of his mercy.* It is often associated with seeing God's grace going only to the elect,* God's covenant people. Sometimes it is called Federal Theology. (See also Covenant of Grace; Covenant of Redemption; Covenant of Works.)

CREATION. (1) The teaching that God made everything that is. Gen. 1 2, Jn. 1:3 and many other Scriptures clearly teach this. (2) It is also the term used for that which God made. (See also Evolution; Theistic Evolution.)

CREATIONISM. (1) A teaching about the beginning of each person's soul.* It says that God creates each new soul out of nothing at the time he gives it a body. Two opposite views are Traducianism* (souls come from parents) and Pre-existence of souls* (souls are alive before being put into bodies). (2) It is also a view about the beginning of the world. It teaches that God made everything there is. The opposite view is evolution.* (See also Creation; Evolution; Pre-existence of Souls; Theistic Evolution; Traducianism.)

CREED. (From Latin: credo, I believe.) A statement or summary of important beliefs. It can be made by a person, a church* or a denomination* (a group of churches who agree on certain beliefs). (See also Catechism; Orthodox, Orthodoxy.)

CRISIS THEOLOGY. (SEE NEO-ORTHODOXY.)

CRITICISM, BIBLICAL. "Criticism" refers to evaluation. (1) It is a broad term used for many methods of biblical interpretation. It asks questions about the Bible that would be asked of other writings. (2) It can be another name for higher criticism.* (See also Criticism, Higher.)

CRITICISM, FORM. The study of the types of stories (oral forms) used in the Bible, especially the Gospels.* It is based on the belief that the gospel was first told orally. Those oral stories were later written down in the form we have them today by the authors. Examples of forms are parables, hymns, legends, etc. The goal of form criticism is to discover the first oral forms. Then we will be able to discover how the authors changed the stories and for what reason. Form critics believe that will help us interpret the Bible better. (See also Criticism, Higher.)

CRITICISM, HIGHER. The part of biblical criticism* that asks questions of the Bible that would be asked of other writings. It deals with questions like: (1) Who is the author? (2) When was it written? (3) What type of literature is it? (4) What other sources did the author use? (5) Is it really true? It is often associated only with the liberal theolo-gies.* However, it is used at least in part by everyone. It is contrasted with "lower," or "textual criticism"* which deals with the texts alone. (See also Criticism, Textual.)

CRITICISM, LOWER. (SEE CRITICISM, TEXTUAL.)

CRITICISM, REDACTION. A method of biblical criticism* that tries to find the intention of an editor. First, it tries to find the sources that were used. Second, it tries to find how the sources were changed according to the editor's purpose. Since the Bible never says there was an editor, it is an area in which we must move with caution. (See also Criticism, Higher; Demythologization; Documentary Hypothesis; Synoptic Problem.)

CRITICISM, TEXTUAL. It is the study that deals with the correct Bible text. The first goal is to find the words of the original text. The second goal is to find how we got the words we have now. It tries to get rid of the errors that may have come into the copies in different ways. It is often called "lower criticism" to separate it from "higher criticism"* (all other types of criticism). (See also Criticism, Higher.)

CROSS. (1) The pieces of wood that Christ was crucified* upon. (2) It is used in the Bible to mean Christ's death, crucifixion, the work he did on the cross, and the whole Christian message. (3) Believers are also called to "take up your cross" (Matt. 16:24). This is a call to commitment. (See also Crucifixion.)

CRUCIFIXION. (From Latin: crux, cross.) Putting a person to death by nailing or tying them to a cross* and leaving them there until they die. It was the worst way a person was killed in the Roman Empire. This was the way Christ died. In the NT, it became one of the words that summarized the gospel.* (See also Cross; Passion of Christ.)

CULT. (From Latin: cultus, worship.) A group which teaches something different from the Bible or what is commonly believed by Christians. There are many characteristics of a cult. Not all of these are necessarily true of every cult. (1) A group organized around a strong leader. The leader is often very strict. (2) They believe they are the only group which teaches truth.* (3) They make their followers obey many rules (legalism*). (4) They emphasize feelings and emotions more than truth. (5) They reject the values of their culture.* Examples of cults are Jehovah's Witnesses and Mormons. It is a very negative term and difficult to define. Sometimes it is called a sect.* (See also Heresy; Sect.)

CULTURE. The way of thinking and actions of a group of people that makes them different from other groups. It includes beliefs, customs, values, actions, what they make, etc. It is important for theology because the gospel* must be told to different cultures in a way they can each understand. (See also Contextualization, World View.)

DAY. In the Bible it can be used in many ways. (1) It can be the hours of daylight (Jn. 11:9). (2) It is most often 24 hours measured from sunset to sunset (Lev. 23:32). (3) It also can be a longer period of time (Jn. 8:56; Gen. 5:4). (4) It can be used as a symbol of good as opposed to evil (1 Thess. 5:5 8). (5) It also can be the time of God's judgment in the future (Isa. 2:12). (See also Day of the Lord; Last Day(s).)

DAY OF ATONEMENT. The day of the year on which the OT high priest* did religious ceremonies to forgive* the sins of all the people of Israel. Lev. 16 explains the practice. Two goats were used. The high priest sacrificed* the first as a sin offering. The other was a "scapegoat,"* taking the sins of the people away never to be seen again. (See also Scapegoat; Propitiation; Atonement; High Priest.)

DAY OF THE LORD. A time in the future when Christ will return (Phil. 1:6). It will be a time of judgment* for the sin of both individuals and nations (Amos 5:18 20;

Joel 2:31). It also will be a time of great blessing* for God's people (Amos 9:11-15; Zeph. 3:9-20). It is also called the Day of Christ or the Day of God. (See also Eschatology; Second Coming of Christ.)

DEACON, DEACONESS. (From Greek: diakoneo, to serve.) One of two biblical offices* in a local church.* In the NT they were people who took care of the needs of the people in the church. The church chose and appointed them. The qualities they must have are listed in I Tim. 3:8-13. (See also Elder; Offices, Church.)

DEAD SEA SCROLLS. The copies of the Bible* and other writings found since 1947 in caves near the Dead Sea, especially at Qumran. They are the oldest copies of the OT that have been ever been found. The Essenes probably wrote them close to the time of Christ. They have helped scholars understand more about the Bible.

DEATH. The main idea is separation as opposed to the end of life. (1) It usually means the end of physical life, the separation of the soul* and body. (2) It also can refer to spiritual death,* the separation from God that is true of unbelievers now. (3) It also can refer to second death,* separation from God forever. (See also Death, Eternal; Death, The First; Death, The Second; Death, Spiritual.)

DEATH, ETERNAL. The complete separation of the wicked from God forever. It is the result of living apart from God. It is death that never ends. (See also Death, The Second.)

DEATH, SPIRITUAL. Being separate from God. All unbelievers are now spiritually dead. Those who die as unbelievers will be spiritually dead forever (eternal death*). (See also Death, the Second; Death, Eternal.)

DEATH, THE FIRST. The end of physical life. The first death happens for both believers and unbelievers. It is different from the second death* which is only for unbelievers. (See also Death, The Second.)

DEATH, THE SECOND. The separation of the wicked from God that will last forever. It is mentioned in Rev. 2:11; 20:6, 14; 21:8. It is also called the "lake of fire."* Believers do not need to be afraid of it. They will live forever with God. (See also Death, Eternal; Death, Spiritual; Lake of Fire.)

DECALOGUE. (From Greek: deka, ten and logos, word.) The ten commandments which God gave Moses in Exod. 20:3 17.

DECREE. A rule or law given by a king or ruler. In theology, it refers to God's plan for all of history. It was made before the beginning of the world. It includes every event in history, even the free* actions of humans. It even includes sin.* Because of that, there is much discus-sion about the nature of decree. (See also Infralapsarian; Sovereignty; Supralapsarian.)

DEISM. (From Latin: deus, God.) The belief that God created* the world but since then has left it alone. He set the world in motion but does not interrupt it now. He keeps creation running by the laws of science. Therefore, there are no miracles.* It says we can know God only through reason. (See also Providence; Theism.)

DEITY OF CHRIST. (From Latin: deus, God.) The idea that Jesus is fully God.* He is God in the same way that God the Father is God. (See also Christology; Trinity.)

DELIVERANCE, DELIVERER. (From Latin: de-, from, and liberare, to set free.) To rescue, save from something bad. (1) The OT uses it mostly for God saving his people from some danger here on earth. (2) The NT uses it for Jesus saving* people from sin. (3) In theology it is also used for rescuing from the power of Satan* or demons.* (See also Demons, Demon Possession; Redeemer; Salvation.)

DELUGE. The big flood of Gen. 7 when only Noah and his family were saved.

DEMONS, DEMON POSSESSION. (From Greek: daimon, demon.) Evil spirits who work for Satan,* the devil. They are angels* who have chosen to sin* and who now do evil. "Possession" is when a demon lives in a person and controls them. (See also Exorcism; Satan.)

DEMYTHOLOGIZATION. The theological method developed by Rudolf Bultmann (1884-1976), a German NT theologian. It is a method of interpreting the Bible. The goal is to free the message of the gospel* from its ancient world view. It is based on the belief that the Bible

is just the human expression of their experience with God.
It is not God's revelation* of himself. It says the Bible
expresses their experience with God in such primitive
thoughts, "myths",* as angels* and demons,* heaven*
above and hell* below the earth, dying and rising gods,
etc. Therefore, we must not interpret them literally.*
Instead, they say we must take these images and realize
that they just reflected the ancient world view and did not
really happen. Bultmann says we must reinter-pret them
from an existential* or personal point of view. The final
step is discovering the experience with God that they
describe. (See also Existential, Existentialism;
Hermeneutics; Myth; Neo-Orthodoxy.)

DENOMINATION. A group of local churches* who
work together and are organized together because they
believe the same things. They also usually have the same
practices, form of church government* (polity) and
traditions.* (See also Church.)

DEPRAVITY, TOTAL. (SEE TOTAL DEPRAVITY.)

DESIGN ARGUMENT. (SEE TELEOLOGICAL
ARGUMENT.)

DETERMINISM. (From Latin: determinare, to limit.)
The belief that everything that happens has a cause.
Everything is fixed or decided ahead of time. Some
believe that things are fixed by laws of nature.* Strict
determinism rules out human freedom.* Theological
determinism believes they are fixed by the will of God.*
Acts 2:23 shows that some things happen because of God's

determined plan. There is much dis-agreement about the limits of determinism. Most theologians believe in some form of concursus* (God works with the free actions of his creatures). (See also Freedom, Free Will; Decree; Concursus.)

DEVIL. (SEE SATAN.)

DIALECTIC THEOLOGY. (From Greek: dealectike, the art of speech, conversation, debate.) Another name for neo orthodox* theology. "Dialectic" refers to a conversation between two people or groups of people who are usually opposed to each other. In theology, "dialectic" refers to the conversation between God and his people. (See also Neo Orthodoxy.)

DICHOTOMY. (From Greek: dicha, in two, and temnein, cut.) Dividing something into two parts. In theology, it is used for the view that humans are made up of two parts: body (material) and soul* (immaterial). (See also Trichotomy.)

DISCIPLE. (From Latin: discipulus, learner.) A person who learns from or follows another. (1) It refers to those who are committed to follow Jesus as their master. (2) It also can refer specifically to the twelve men Jesus chose to follow Him. (See also Apostle.)

DISCIPLINE, CHURCH. The action of the church in guiding each member. It usually means correcting and even punishing sinful believers. The goal should always be holiness* and purity. It tries to restore the believer, bring them back into the fellowship* of the church. It is based on the holiness of God. Key passages about discipline are Matt. 18:15 17 and 1 Cor. 5:13. (See also Excommunication.)

DISPENSATION. The management and plan of a household. In theology it means the different ways God carries out his plan for the world. (See also Dispensational Theology.)

DISPENSATIONAL THEOLOGY. Belief that God works out his plan for the world in different ways at different times. It has three main points. (1) Our interpretation of the Bible must be controlled by the intent of the original author (literalism*). (2) The Church is something new that began at Pentecost.* (3) There will be a future for Israel as a nation in the millennium* (1000 year rule of Christ on earth). (See also Literalism; Millennium; Pentecost.)

DIVINE. (From Latin: deus, God.) To be God* or a god. It is used of both the true God of the Bible or false gods that are worshipped* by unbelievers. (See also Deity of Christ.)

DOCETISM. (From Greek: dokein, to seem.) A view of Christ started in the second century. It teaches that Jesus was just God* and only "seemed" to be human. They say that God could not suffer, so Christ only looked like he was suffering. This view is not accepted by orthodox* Christians today. (See also Christology; Hypostatic Union; Impassibility.)

DOCTRINE. (From Latin: docere, to teach.) A belief or teaching of the Bible in an area of theology.* For example, it might be a teaching about the nature of God or how to be saved. (See also Systematic Theology.)

DOCUMENTARY HYPOTHESIS. A theory about the who wrote the first five books of the Bible. It says Moses did not write them. Instead, they were written by several editors over a period of time using several different books. Those other books were written by people traditionally called J, E, D, and P. Today, the study about the first five books of the OT is much more complex than this. It is also called the Wellhausen Theory. (See also Criticism, Redaction.)

DOGMA. (Greek word: dogma, decision or command.) In theology, the official teaching of the church. It carries authority.* It often has a negative, legalistic* meaning today, so it is not used often. (See also Dogmatics.)

DOGMATICS. (Greek word: dogma, decision or command.) The logical, orderly study of the teachings of the Bible. It is another name for systematic theology.* (See also Dogma; Systematic Theology.)

DOMINION. (From Latin: dominari, to rule.) To rule, lead or have authority. (1) God has dominion over everything. However, he commanded Adam and Eve to have dominion also over all he created in Gen. 1:28. (2) It is also the name for a theology which is also called "Theonomy."* (See also Creation; Theonomy.)

DOUBLE PREDESTINATION. The belief that God has chosen both some people to be saved* and some to be condemned.* The actions of humans do not matter at all. It is only God's choice. (See also Election; Predestination; Preterition; Reprobation.)

DOXOLOGY. (From Greek: doxa, glory.) A giving of praise* to God. It is worshipping* all three persons of the Trinity.* It often refers to a certain fixed wording. Biblical examples are Lk. 2:14 and Rom. 11:33-36. (See also Praise.)

DUALISM. (From Latin: duo, two.) The theory that there are two opposite powers in the world or in a certain situation. There are many different forms of it. (1) God and Satan* the Bible denies this because they are not equal powers. (2) Mind and body an understanding of persons that sees a distinction between the material (body) and the immaterial (soul*) parts of a person. It sometimes becomes a non-biblical view when it says that mind is good and body is evil. (3) There are other dualisms also such as ideas and objects. (See also Gnosticism; Dichotomy.)

DYNAMIC PRESENCE. A view of the Lord's Supper.* It teaches that the bread and wine are not changed, but Christ is spiritually present in the service. It is taught by Calvinism* and in many Reformed* churches. It is a middle view between Real Presence* and Memorialism* views. (See also Lord's Supper; Memorialism; Real Presence; Transubstantiation.)

EASTER. The holiday that celebrates the day Jesus rose from the dead. (See also Resurrection of Christ.)

EASTERN ORTHODOX CHURCH. (SEE ORTHODOX CHURCH.)

ECCLESIA. (From Greek: ekklesia, church, assembly.) Greek word for church* meaning the gathering of Christians. (See also Church.)

ECCLESIOLOGY. (From Greek: ekklesia, church, assembly, and logos, word.) The doctrine of the church.* It includes topics like what the church is, what it is to do, how to be a part of it, and how to organize it. It also includes teaching about baptism* and the Lord's Supper.* (See also Church.)

ECONOMIC VIEW OF THE TRINITY. A way of looking at the three persons* in the one God. It focuses on the different works or respon-sibilities of each. It also looks at the different ways the three persons are made known. Hippolytus (c. 170-236) of Rome and Tertullian (c. 155-220) of North Africa started this view. (See also Trinity.)

ECUMENICAL, ECUMENISM. (From Greek: oikoumene, whole world that people live in.) Trying to unify* churches together. In the early church it refers to meetings to which people from all over the world came. Today it refers to a movement that tries to unify believers. It tries to combine churches together or encourage them to work together. (See also Church; Unity.)

EDIFICATION, EDIFY. (From Latin: aedificare, to build [a house].) (1) It means helping believers to grow in faith.* (2) It means spiritually strengthening a church. (See also Church; Renewal.)

EFFECTUAL CALLING. The special call* of God. The ones whom he calls always believe in the gospel* and are saved.* God calls only those whom he has chosen to save. Reformed theology* teaches this view. It is related to efficacious grace.* (See also Efficacious Grace; Elect; Election.)

EFFICACIOUS GRACE. The grace* of God that always does what he plans for it to do. It is the view that those God has chosen will believe and they will be saved and made like Christ. God's grace will be powerful in changing a person's life to be like Christ. What God decides to do will always happen. It is sometimes called irresistible grace.* Calvinism* and Reformed Theology* teaches this view. (See also Election; Irresistible Grace.)

EFFUSION. (SEE POURING.)

EISEGESIS. (From Greek: eisegesis, to read into.) The error of letting our own prejudices affect our interpretation of the Bible. It is the opposite of exegesis,* that is, finding the meaning that is already there. (See also Exegesis; Hermeneutics.)

EL SHADDAI. (From Hebrew: el, God, and shaddai, mountain.) A name for God meaning power. It is often translated "God Almighty" in English. (See also

Omnipotence; Sovereignty.)

ELDER. In the Bible it means several different things.
(1) In the OT, it was an older man who is a leader of a
family or town. (2) In the Gospels,* it was the group of
leaders who led the Jewish* people. (3) In the early
church, it was one of two biblical offices.* Elders in this
last sense are those who lead the church.* The qualities
they must have are listed in I Tim. 3:1-13 and Tit. 1:5-9.
(See also Deacon, Deaconess; Officer, Church.)

ELECT. (From Latin: electus, to pick out, to choose.)
Either those people chosen by God in a special way (as a
noun) or the choosing itself (as a verb). It can refer to
individuals or groups (i.e. Israel). The choosing can be for
service, blessing,* or especially for salvation.* (See also
Predestination.)

ELECTION. (From Latin: electus, to pick out, to
choose.) The special decision of God in choosing
individuals or groups of people (i.e. Israel). It can be for
service, blessing* or especially for salvation.*
Arminian-ism* says God knows ahead of time who will
believe and chooses to give them the blessings of
salvation. Reformed/Calvinism* says God chooses based
on his decision alone and then those people believe.
Unconditional election is the "U" in Calvinism's TULIP.*
(See also Predestination; TULIP.)

ELOHIM. (Plural of the Hebrew word: el, God.) A
general name for a god. It is used for both pagan gods and
the true God of Israel. When it refers to the true God, it

speaks of the One who is the Creator,* separate from the creature.

EMANATION. (From Latin: emanatus, to flow out.) (1) Something that flows out, usually of God. It is a term used for a view of creation.* It says that everything flowed out of God. He took a piece of himself and made the world out of it. He did not create it ex nihilo* (out of nothing). (2) It is also used for a Gnostic* answer to the problem of evil. They say there were some things that flowed out (emanated) and then more things flowed out of that, etc. Those became more and more physical, material (which they believe is evil). This then became the source of evil. (See also Creation; Gnosticism.)

EMMANUEL. (SEE IMMANUEL.)

EMPIRICISM. (From Greek: empeiria, experience.) The view that all knowledge comes from our senses or our experience. It is the basis of some theologies and philosophies. The opposite view is rationalism,* the belief that knowledge comes from reason alone, without relying on the senses. (See also Rationalism; Epistemology.)

ENTIRE SANCTIFICATION. The Wesleyan* teaching that a person can become completely holy* in this life. We are made holy by grace* through faith, not by works. It is often defined as "perfect love." Some even say it means never to sin.* It is also called perfectionism* or "second blessing."* Most other theologies do not believe it can happen in this life. (See also Good Works; Holy,

Holiness; Perfectionism; Sanctification; Second Blessing; Wesleyan.)

EPIPHANY. (From Greek: epiphaneia, uncover or reveal.) It refers to the coming of Christ. (1) It can be used of either his first or second coming.* (2) It is also a Christian holiday (Jan. 6). (See also Advent; Incarnation; Second Coming.)

EPISCOPAL GOVERNMENT. (From Greek: episkopos, bishop, over-seer.) A way that some churches are organized. Authority* is given to bishops* who rule over the churches. Its model is that James, Timothy and Titus were leaders of many churches. These bishops are seen as following in a line from the apostles.* The two other offices of the church are priests* and deacons.* (See also Bishop; Congregationalism; Government, Church; Presbyterian Government.)

EPISTEMOLOGY. (From Greek: episteme, knowledge, and logos, word.) The study of knowledge. It explores what we know and how we know it. In religion, it includes knowing God. (See also Metaphysics; Philosophy.)

EPISTLE. (From Greek: epistole, letter.) The name used for the books of the NT which were written as letters. Usually they are divided into the Pauline and "catholic,"* or general epistles. (See also Catholic.)

ESCHATOLOGY. (From Greek: eschatos, last and logos, word.) The part of theology* that deals with the last things, the end of the age,* the fu-ture. It includes topics like what happens after death,* the return of Christ, the life that will go on forever, and the final working out of God's plan. It is often called general eschatology to contrast it with individual eschatology.* (See also Eschatology, Individual; Inaugurated Eschatology; Realized Eschatology.)

ESCHATOLOGY, INDIVIDUAL. The study of what happens to each person after this life. It is the future events of one person, not the world as a whole ("general eschatology"). It includes death,* resurrection of the body,* and the time between them (intermediate state*). (See also Eschatology.)

ESSENCE. (From Latin: esse, to be.) That which is truly real; the nature of something. It is that which makes a thing what it is. It is the sum total of all its attributes. (See also Attributes of God.)

ETERNAL DEATH. (SEE DEATH, ETERNAL.)

ETERNAL DESTINY. The situation toward which a person is heading after this life. That place may be either with God (heaven*) or apart from God (hell*) forever. The result is decided by a person's relationship with Christ. (See also Final State; Heaven; Hell.)

ETERNAL GENERATION. A view of the relationship of God the Father and God the Son. It says that the Son has always been the Son of God,* even before he came to earth. The Son has exactly the same nature as the Father because it always comes from the Father. It is not a matter of creation. Instead, it is a giving of personhood that never began and never ends. There was never a time when the Son did not exist. (See also Only Begotten; Pre-Existence of Christ.)

ETERNAL LIFE. Life with God that goes on forever for believers. It is the blessing of salvation.* Jn. 17:3 describes it as knowing God and Jesus. It will be a much better quality of life than here on earth. (See also Heaven.)

ETERNAL SECURITY. The teaching that once a person is truly saved they will never lose their salvation.* God will keep them secure. He will help that person keep on being faithful (perseverance*). It is a Calvinist* teaching. (See also Assurance; Perseverance.)

ETERNAL STATE. (SEE FINAL STATE.)

ETERNITY. Apart from and above time; without beginning or end. Sometimes it refers to being outside of time. Other times it is used to describe God because he has no beginning or end and is apart from time. (See also Attributes of God.)

ETHICS. (From Greek: ethikos, character, custom.) In general, it is the rules or principles by which we guide our lives (morality*). In philosophy,* it is the study of the nature of morality or moral acts. It is the study of what makes an action good or bad. In a Christian ethic, the basis for good or bad is found in the will of God.* (See also Morality.)

EUCHARIST. (SEE LORD'S SUPPER.)

EUTYCHIANISM. (SEE MONOPHYSITISM.)

EVANGELICAL, EVANGELICALISM. (From Greek: euangelion, good news, gospel.) The belief in and speaking to others about the good news of Jesus. Though there is no formal statement of beliefs, they usually believe several truths. There are two main teachings. (1) Every person needs to be saved. Salvation* comes only through Christ's substitutionary* death on the cross* to pay for our sin. That is a result of God's grace* alone. People receive it through faith.* (2) The Bible is the Word of God* and completely truthful. It is the highest authority* in a believer's life. It is higher than the church, reason, or anything else. They also teach other orthodox* truths which have been held through history. For example, they believe there are three persons in the one God (Trinity*). Therefore, both Jesus and the Holy Spirit are God. Also, Jesus was born of a virgin,* died on a cross for human sin* and bodily rose from the dead. He will return bodily and personally to judge* all humanity at the end of the age.* Also, the miracles* of the Bible are true. An opposite view is theological liberalism.* (See also Fundamentalism; Liberalism, Theological; Orthodox, Orthodoxy.)

EVANGELISM. (From Greek: euangelion, good news, gospel.) Telling the good news of the gospel* to other people. It is done with the goal of leading the person to salvation* through belief in Jesus. All believers are commanded to tell others the gospel (Matt. 28:18 20; Acts 1:8). (See also Church; Witness, Testimony.)

EVANGELIST. (From Greek: euangelistes, to announce or bring good news.) A person who tells the good news of the gospel* to others. It is usually those who have special abilities or gifts in evangelism* (Eph. 4:11). (See also Evangelism; Spiritual Gifts.)

EVERLASTING LIFE. (SEE ETERNAL LIFE.)

EVIL. That which is opposite of God's best. It includes both moral evil* (that which is sinful) and natural evil* (harmful things in creation). (See also Moral Evil; Natural Evil.)

EVOLUTION. (1) The belief that there is change over time. It is the process of change from one form into another one. (2) It is also the belief that all life is related to each other because of a common beginning. This is a scientific theory that simple living things became more complex over time. It is a view of how the world began. It is often taught in opposition to the view that God created* the world. (3) It is also a view that all change happens by random chance. There is no one who is directing the world. This is a world view which is opposed to Christianity. This view rules out both creation* and providence.* (See also Creation; Providence; Determinism; Theistic Evolution.)

EX CATHEDRA. (Latin words: ex cathedra, from the

throne, chair.) A statement made by the Pope* when he is officially acting as leader of the church. He makes these statements specifically as "ex cathedra" statements. They are about morals and faith. Roman Catholics* believe them to be infallible,* without error. This does not apply to the many other things a Pope might say at other times. (See also Catholicism, Roman; Infallibility, Papal; Pope.)

EX NIHILO, CREATIO. (Latin words: creatio ex nihilo, creation out of nothing.) The teaching that God created* the world out of nothing. There was no material there before he created the world. (See also Creation.)

EX OPERE OPERATO. (Latin words: ex opere operato, from the action done.) The Roman Catholic* teaching that grace* is given to whoever participates in the sacraments.* The goodness of the person who gives or receives the sacrament does not affect the grace given. The grace can be stopped only if it is actively hindered. (See also Sacrament.)

EXCOMMUNICATION. Cutting off or removing a person from the fellowship* of a church. It is the end of the process of church discipline* if there has been no repentance* (Matt. 18). The purpose is so the person will repent and be sorry for sin. It is also done to keep the church pure. In the Roman Catholic Church,* excommunication is believed to include the loss of salvation.* (See also Discipline, Church.)

EXEGESIS. (Greek word: exegesis, explanation.) The method of interpreting the Bible. It tries to discover the sense of Scripture. The goal is to find the author's meaning. It is done by finding the meaning from the Bible that is already there; it is not reading our understanding into it (eisegesis*). It is based on the grammatical and historical theory of interpretation. (See also Eisegesis; Hermeneutics.)

EXISTENTIAL, EXISTENTIALISM. The common view of existentialists is that truth comes in real life experiences rather than general statements. It focuses on the individual's attempt to discover truth which helps in the struggles of every day life. What is important is what I have experienced rather than what others say is true. Truth* demands personal involvement. For example, a person learns about love only by loving someone else. Individual freedom, responsibility and the uncertainty of life are basic concepts. (See also Neo-Orthodoxy.)

EXORCISM. (From Greek: exorkizein, to send away an evil spirit.) The sending of evil spirits (demons*) out of a person. It was a part of Jesus' ministry (Mk. 1:21 34). (See also Demons, Demon Possession.)

EXPIATION. To cancel and cleanse from sin.* Some people say that Christ's death just cancelled our sin. It is less complete than propitiation* which means to take away God's wrath. (See also Atone-ment; Propitiation.)

FAITH. (From Latin: fides, confidence, trust.) The belief or trust in someone or something. In theology, it is knowing Jesus and being certain that he is God's Son and the Savior.* It is also committing oneself to Jesus as the only way to come to God. It is believing that God will keep his promise to give eternal life* to those who trust in Jesus. (See also Conversion; Lordship Salvation; Salvation.)

FALL OF MAN, THE. The first time Adam and Eve disobeyed God in the garden (Gen. 3). It led to many terrible results for every human being. Adam and Eve and all humans afterwards were now separated from God. (See also Imputation; Original Sin.)

FAST, FASTING. Choosing not to eat some or all food for a certain period of time. It is usually done for religious reasons. It was a practice in both the OT and NT (Neh. 1:4; Acts 13:3).

FATE, FATALISM. The belief that a force controls everything that happens. This force is not personal and therefore is not God. There is nothing anyone can do to change what will happen. There is no purpose to anything. God's providence* is the opposite because God is personal and guides everything to his purpose. (See Determinism; Providence.)

FEDERAL HEADSHIP. (From Latin: foedus, covenant.) The view of Covenant* (or Federal) Theology. Adam was appointed by God and acted as representative, head, of the whole human race when he sinned. Therefore, all people share in the results of his sin. Christ, the Second Adam, was also appointed by God. He acted as representative, head, of the race of believers when he obeyed God. Therefore, all believers share in the results of his life. Its support is Rom. 5:15-21 and I Cor. 15:22. (See also Covenant Theology.)

FEDERAL THEOLOGY. (SEE COVENANT THEOLOGY.)

FELLOWSHIP. A term used for the close relationship between believers. The Greek word is koinonia, meaning "to share in." It is shown in encouraging, comforting and sharing what you have, including money, with others. It is the close friendship between those who love Jesus.

FIDEISM. (From Latin: fides, faith.) Most often it means one believes in Christian truths just because of faith.* We believe only because of the Holy Spirit, for no other reason. It says a person cannot prove things are true by reason alone. It usually has a negative meaning. (See also Faith.)

FILIOQUE. (Latin word: filioque, and the Son.) A phrase in the Western version of the Nicene Creed. It says that the Holy Spirit* came out (proceeded) from the Father "and the Son." The main point of the discussion is if Jesus is fully God. A major disagreement started over this phrase. This was because the Eastern Orthodox* Church believed the Son was subordinate* to the Father. As a result, the Eastern and Western (Roman Catholic*) churches separated from each other over this doctrine in 1054. It is also called "Procession of the Spirit." (See also Deity of Christ; Trinity.)

FILLED WITH THE SPIRIT. The Holy Spirit giving

power to and directing a believer. A person is so filled with the things of God that the focus of life is spiritual things. It is commanded in Eph. 5:18. Believers should be filled with the Spirit continually as they grow in faith. It is different from baptism in the Spirit* which happens once at conversion.* There is much debate on what exactly the filling of the Spirit means. (See also Baptism In/Of/With the Holy Spirit; Holy Spirit.)

FINAL STATE. The place where a person will go following being raised after death.* That place may be either with God (heaven*) or apart from God (hell*). The result is decided by one's relationship with Christ. (See Eternal Destiny; Heaven; Hell.)

FLESH, FLESHLY. (1) Literally, the physical body of a person that is different from the soul.* (2) It is also used, especially by Paul, to mean the sinful* part of a person. This is also the sinful actions that come out of the it. "Fleshly," like "carnal," is used to speak of persons who are doing things on their own power as opposed to the power of the Spirit. (3) It is also used to speak of Christ as a human. This does not have a sinful sense. (See also Christology; Sin.)

FOREKNOWLEDGE. God knows everything that will happen in the future. (See also Omniscience; Predestination.)

FOREORDINATION. (SEE PREDESTINATION.)

FORGIVENESS. Not to hold a person's sin* against

them. It is the pardon of the wrong a person has done and removal of the guilt. Because of that, the two can be friends again. It is offered by God through Jesus to all who will repent* and receive it. Believers are also called to forgive others. (See also Guilt; Reconciliation.)

FORM CRITICISM. (SEE CRITICISM, FORM.)

FREE WILL. (SEE FREEDOM.)

FREEDOM, FREE WILL, FREEDOM OF THE WILL. The view that a person makes their own choices about what they will do. Their actions are not determined by anything or anyone else. It often includes the idea that people are also responsible for their actions. Phlm. 14 and Jn. 7:17 teach that humans have power of choice. It is often taught as the opposite of determinism* or fatalism.* (See also Determinism; Fate, Fatalism; Decree; Predestination.)

FRUIT OF THE SPIRIT. The spiritual character in a believer that is the result of the Holy Spirit's work. Gal. 5:22 23 lists the fruit. Love,* joy* and peace are examples.

FUNDAMENTALISM. (From Latin: fundus, bottom.) (1) A theological movement that started in the United States in the 1920's. It teaches the orthodox* truths as evangelicals.* However, it was distinct because it stood strongly against and tried to separate from all forms of liberalism.* (2) It is also a theology. The "fundamentals" or basic beliefs are several. (a) The Bible is inerrant,* without error. (b) There is one God in three persons (Trinity*). (c) Christ is fully God and fully human. He was born of a virgin.* (d) Humans were created by God. They sinned. (e) Christ died on the cross to take the penalty for human sin. (f) Christ bodily rose from the dead and went up into heaven. (g) God makes new (regenerates*) those who believe in Jesus. (h) Christ will bodily return at any time. (i) All people will be raised after death. They will be in heaven* or hell* forever. (3) It also refers to an attitude of fundamentalism. It is an attitude of separation and is critical of anything different. They will not compromise. This is used in a negative way of many types of groups. (See also Evangelical, Evangelicalism; Liberalism, Theological; Orthodoxy.)

FUTURE STATE. A person's situation after death. It includes the time both from death to resurrection* (intermediate state*) and after that (final state*). (See also Eternal State; Final State; Intermediate State.)

GEHENNA. (Greek from Aramaic: gehinnam, Valley of Hinnom.) A place outside Jerusalem where children had been sacrificed (2 Ki. 16:3). The word "Gehenna" began to be used to refer to hell, the place of punishment for the wicked (Matt. 25:41). It has the idea of fire and burning. (See also Hades, Sheol; Hell.)

GENERAL REVELATION. (SEE REVELATION, GENERAL.)

GENTILES. (From Latin: gentilis, foreigner.) Everyone who is not a Jew* by race. (See also Jew.)

GIFTS, SPIRITUAL. (SEE SPIRITUAL GIFTS.)

GLORIFICATION. (From Latin: gloria, glory, and facere, to make.) The final step of the salvation* process. It is at the end of the age* when the believer will be given a new body and be made completely holy.* They will be in the presence of Christ. There will be no more death. (See also Heaven; Justification, Justify; Sanctification.)

GLORY. The brightness, greatness, beauty, or perfection of God which can be seen. It is the combination of all the qualities of God. It is also used to mean the human response of honoring God for his glory. (See also Attributes of God.)

GLOSSOLALIA. (SEE TONGUES.)

GNOSTICISM. (From Greek: gnosis, knowledge.) A religion that began during the early years of Christianity. Gnostics say that people are saved by a special knowledge from God apart from the gospel.* Its main teachings are: (1) There is a war going on between the spiritual world and the physical world. (2) Knowledge and the mind are good but the body and everything physical is evil. (3) Jesus did not really become human and did not suffer. (See also Dualism.)

GOD. The personal supreme being who created the universe, now controls and cares for it, and is redeeming his people. The Westminster Catechism defines him as, "a spirit, infinite, eternal and unchangeable in his being, wisdom,* power, holiness,* justice,* goodness and

truth."* He is the one whom believers worship,* love*
and serve. He has a plan for the world and is working it
out. In the Bible, God is described as three persons in one
God (Trinity*). (See also Attributes of God; Decree;
Theology Proper; Trinity.)

GODLINESS. Being like God in character. It describes
the person who does the things God wants and has
attitudes like God's. The Holy Spirit gives believers the
power to be godly. (See also Fruit of the Spirit; Imitation
of Christ.)

GOOD WORKS. Positive actions done by people. It is
used in two ways. (1) It has a positive meaning. Believers
are commanded to obey* God. They do these acts by the
power of God's grace. They do them because they love
God (Eph. 2:10). (2) It also has a negative meaning. It is
the acts people do to try to earn God's favor or salvation*
apart from Christ. These works do not please God. (See
also Work, Works.)

GOSPEL. (1) The "good news" of what God has done for
us in Jesus. It is the message that God sent his Son, Jesus,
to die and be raised to take away the sins* of the world. It
is for all who believe in Jesus. (2) The first four books of
the NT are also called Gospels. (See also Salvation.)

GOVERNMENT, DIVINE. A term used to speak of
God guiding his creation to his purposes for it. It is part of
providence,* his care for his creation.* (See also
Providence.)

GOVERNMENTAL THEORY OF THE ATONEMENT. (SEE ATONE-MENT, GOVERNMENTAL.)

GRACE. (From Latin: gratia, pleasing, favor.) The love* and goodness of God given to those who do not deserve it. It is God's forgiveness* of sinners because of Jesus. There is nothing we can do to earn it; it is free. It especially refers to the people he chose (elects*) and the promises he made to different groups of people (covenants*). (See also Covenant; Election.)

GRACE, COMMON. (SEE COMMON GRACE.)

GRACE, PREVENIENT. (SEE PREVENIENT GRACE.)

GREAT COMMISSION. The command to take the gospel* to all nations. In Matt. 28:19 20 and other NT passages, Jesus told the disciples to preach the gospel to the whole world. (See also Evangelism; Mission, Missions, Missiology.)

GREAT TRIBULATION. The time at the end of this age* when there will be more suffering than any other time. It is a time when God's wrath will be poured out. The Antichrist* will rule during that time. The book of Revelation speaks a lot about the Great Tribulation. People have many different views about how long it will be; some say seven years and others say just a period of time. There are also different views about if the church will go through it. (See also Antichrist; Eschatology;

Tribulation.)

GREEK ORTHODOX CHURCH. (SEE ORTHODOX CHURCH.)

GROTIAN THEORY. (SEE ATONEMENT, GOVERNMENTAL.)

GUILT. Deserving punishment for doing something wrong or breaking a law, especially God's law. (See also Forgiveness.)

HADES, SHEOL. (Greek word: hades, place of the dead; translation of the Hebrew word: sheol.) Both are names for the place all people go when they die. Specifically, it is (1) the presence of God for believers, and (2) the place of punishment for the unbelievers. It is used in Matt. 11:23 and Lk. 10:15; 16:23. (See also Gehenna; Heaven; Hell.)

HALLELUJAH. (From Hebrew: halal, praise, and Yah, Yahweh.) A command to praise* the Lord. It is a joyful reporting of how great God. It is done while in worship* with other people. Today it is used in most languages of the world to worship God. Alleluia is another way of writing it. (See also Praise.)

HALLOW. To make holy,* honor as holy, or set something apart for religious use. We are told to hallow God's name (Matt. 6:9). (See also Holy, Holiness; Name.)

HALLOWED. It describes the object or person that is

made holy,* honored as holy, or set apart for religious use. (See also Holy, Holiness.)

HAMARTIOLOGY. (From Greek: hamartia, sin and logos, word.) The part of theology that deals with sin.* It includes topics like where sin came from (origin), what it is (nature), and its results. (See also Original Sin; Sin.)

HARDNESS OF HEART. An attitude that will not hear God or respond to him. It is rejecting God and the Bible for a long time. It becomes very difficult for that person to follow God. In theology there are many questions about who does the hardening. Some Calvinists* say it is only God. Some Arminians* say it is only humans. Most people agree that it is some combination of the two. (See also Unbelief.)

HEART. In the Bible, the deepest part of a person. It is what controls a person. It is the place of not only the emotions, but also the will, intel-lect, morals, etc. (See also Soul; Spirit; Will.)

HEAVEN. (1) It is the place where believers go after they die. God is there with them. People are joyful and happy and worship* God there. (2) The place where God lives now is also called "heaven." (3) It is also used for just the sky, the place of the stars. (See also Eternal Life; Hell.)

HEILSGESCHICHTE. (German word: heilsgeschichte, salvation history.) The view that the Bible is a history of God's saving activity. (1) This term is most often used by neo-orthodox* theologians. They believe there is a separate history in which God acts. This is only knowable by faith, not historical methods. They understand the Bible as a whole. Therefore, the details are not important. As a result, they cannot be used to prove certain doctrines.* (2) Other theologians use it to show the reality of how God is at work in history. (See also Hermeneutics; Neo-Orthodoxy.)

HEIR. A person who has the right to receive the property of another person when he dies. The heir is usually a child. Since believers are adopted* as children of God, they are heirs of God. (See also Adoption; In-heritance.)

HELL. It is the place where the wicked will be punished after they die. They will be separated from God. There is much disagreement about what hell will be like. Hades, Gehenna, and Sheol are words sometimes used for hell. (See also Gehenna; Hades, Sheol; Hell.)

HERESY. (From Greek: hairesis, choice, school, sect.) Denying a Chris-tian truth and believing an error. It is a belief or teaching that is against what the Bible or correct theology teaches (orthodox*) (2 Pet. 2:1). (See also Apostasy; Backsliding; Cult; Heterodox; Sect.)

HERMENEUTICS. (From Greek: hermeneuein, to interpret.) The study of principles of interpreting the Bible. The goal is to discover what the meaning of the authors. (See also Allegory; Analogy; Exegesis; Literalism; Symbol.)

HETERODOXY. (SEE ORTHODOX, ORTHODOXY.)

HIGH PRIEST. (1) In the OT, he was the most important of the priests.* (2) By the time of the NT, he held a lot of power in politics also. (3) Jesus is called our High Priest in Hebrews. He offered himself as the sacrifice* for believers and prays* for them, the two jobs of the high priest. (See also Intercession; Offices of Christ; Priest; Sacrifice.)

HIGHER CRITICISM. (SEE CRITICISM, NT, OT.)

HISTORICAL JESUS, THE. A phrase used by theological liberals* in the 19th century and today. They believe he was only human and not divine.* They believe stories and legends began to be told about Jesus. Those stories described him as a god. So they try to use historical methods to discover the "actual Jesus" who lived in the first century. They want to remove the stories or "myths"* about Jesus that his followers told about him that they claim did not really happen. Often they use methods of higher criticism.* They refer to most of what is in the NT as the "Christ of Faith." That includes things like his miracles,* deity,* and bodily resurrection.* They believe the "Christ of Faith" is just a story or legend and never really lived. (See also Criticism, Higher; Liberalism, Theological.)

HISTORICAL THEOLOGY. The study of the history of theology.* It is the study of the development and change of certain doctrines* over the years. For example, historical theology would trace the views of Christ from the early church through the years to today. (See also Biblical Theology; Systematic Theology.)

HOLY GHOST. (SEE HOLY SPIRIT.)

HOLY, HOLINESS. Set apart, separate, pure. A person or object that is separated from sin* unto God. God is perfectly holy. Those who believe in Jesus are also called holy (set apart) and are commanded to live holy (pure) lives. (See also Attributes of God; Sanctification.)

HOLY OF HOLIES. The center part of the temple* or tabernacle.* Inside there was the ark of the covenant,* the cherubim* (statues of angels* made out of wood, covered with gold), and the mercy seat.* God's glory (shekinah*) was there (1 Ki. 8:10-11). Only the high priest* could go through the curtain into it. He could only go in once a year on the Day of Atonement* (Lev. 16). (See also Ark of the Covenant; Mercy Seat; Shekinah; Tabernacle; Temple.)

HOLY SPIRIT. The third person of the Trinity.* He is fully God and is fully personal. He lives in believers and is God's presence in the world today. He gives spiritual gifts* to, fills, and baptizes* believers and convicts* all people of sin and righteousness. (See also Baptism In/Of/With the Spirit; Filled with the Spirit; Fruit of the Spirit; Trinity.)

HOMILETICS. (From Greek: homiletikos, conversation.) The science and art of preaching. It includes both the writing and preaching of sermons. (See also Pastoral Theology.)

HOMOLOGOUMENA. (From Greek: homos, same,

and legein, to say; literally: to agree.) The NT books which everyone agreed should be a part of the Bible. It is contrasted with antilegomena,* those books over which there was disagreement. (See also Antilegomena; Canon.)

HOPE. (1) The attitude of looking forward to good things in the future. Believers believe that God will do what he promises.* We look forward to it with confidence. So we "hope" in the future events that God promised (like the second coming of Christ*). (2) It is also the one in whom we hope. In this sense, God and Jesus are called our hope. (See also Joy.)

HOSANNA. (Greek form of Hebrew word: hosanna, Save us, we ask you.) In the OT it was a cry for help. In the NT it is used to greet the coming of the Messiah.* Today it is used in worship for praise,* joy* or thanks. (See also Praise.)

HUMAN NATURE. That which is shared by all persons. It is what makes every person a human. Examples would be the ability to reason, to choose, to relate to God, etc. (See also Image of God, Imago Dei.)

HUMANISM. The belief or practice that humans are to be highly valued. There are several different types of humanism. (1) Humans are the highest of all beings. Therefore there is no God (atheism*). This is called secular humanism.* (2) Humans are the most important creature even though there may be a higher being (i.e., God). (3) God is the highest being and deserves our highest worship.* However, humans are his most important creation. Therefore, they are not to be wor-shipped, but treated with respect and dignity. This is Christian humanism. (See also Anthropocentric; Secular Humanism.)

HUMILITY. The quality of not thinking too highly of yourself. It is to see yourself in a proper way. God wants us to be humble. The opposite is pride.* (See also Pride.)

HYPOCRISY. (From Greek: hypokrisis, play-acting.) A person who pretends to be something they are not. It is someone who says they love Jesus or tries to act like it, but really does not. (See also Pride.)

HYPOSTASIS. (Greek word: hypostasis, substance, nature, essence, person.) The true inner part of persons* apart from their attributes or qualities. It is used in two ways in theology. (1) It is used with all three persons of the Trinity.* It refers to what is really God apart from his attributes.* (2) It also refers to Christ's two natures (human and God) together in one person. (See also Christology; Hypostatic Union; Trinity.)

HYPOSTATIC UNION. (Greek word: hypostasis, substance, nature, es-sence, person.) Part of the study of Christ. It refers to his two natures (human and God) being united together in one person. When Christ became human, his divine* nature was forever united with his human nature. He is fully God and fully human. (See also Christology; Hypostasis.)

IDENTIFICATION WITH CHRIST. (1) The union of

a believer with Christ. This is a change of position to be placed in the family of Christ. It is taken from the passages which speak of a believer being "in Christ" (Eph. 1:3-14; Rom. 6). It is the result of baptism in the Holy Spirit.* (2) It is also used for a mystical or spiritual union with Christ.* This idea is used by Keswick* theology to speak of Christ taking my place as the director of my life. It is also used by mystics* to speak of actually spiritually becoming a part of Christ. (See also Union with Christ.)

IDOLATRY, IDOL. (From Greek: eidolon, image, form.) The honor or worship* which should be given only to God that is given to something other than God. In the OT, an idol was a physical object often made out of wood or stone. In theology, it is anything that takes the place of God. For example, today idols might be money, family, power, etc. (See also Animism; Image; Polytheism.)

IGNORANCE. (From Latin: in-, not, and gnarus, knowing.) Lack of knowledge. In the Bible, sometimes people sinned because they did not know it was wrong. But it is often treated as less evil than a sin* in which the person knew what they were doing was wrong and did it anyway. (See also Sin.)

ILLUMINATION. (From Latin: in-, in, and luminare, to light.) The Holy Spirit's* work of giving understanding of the Bible. There is disagree-ment about what this means. Some say the Holy Spirit gives all people understanding into the Bible's meaning. Others say he gives only believers understanding of the significance or personal application of the Bible. (See also Hermeneutics; Holy

Spirit.)

IMAGE. (From Latin: imago, image, copy.) Something that looks like another person or thing. It is usually made of a different material (i.e., stone, metal). It has two meanings in theology. (1) It often refers to a physical object that is an idol or god to be worshipped. (2) It also refers to humans made in the image of God.* (See also Idol; Image of God, Imago Dei.)

IMAGE OF GOD, IMAGO DEI. (From Latin: imago, image, copy.) God created humans to be like himself (Gen. 1:26). They are to represent him on earth. There are many ideas about what human characteristics are part of the image. Most people agree that it includes at least being able to think, to choose, to know and love God and others, and being able to use those abilities for God's glory. Christ is also the Image of God (Col. 1:15-20). (See also Anthropology; Human Nature; Image.)

IMITATION OF CHRIST. The goal of trying to live like Jesus. The Bible commands Christians to follow Jesus (Phil. 2:5; 1 Thess. 1:6). We can be like him because we are made in the image of God* and the Holy Spirit lives in us. We are to be like him in areas like humility,* ministry,* and obedience.* (See also Image of God, Imago Dei; Sanctification.)

IMMACULATE CONCEPTION. (From Latin: in-, not, and maculare, to spot, spoil.) The Roman Catholic* belief that Mary, the mother of Jesus, was free from all sin. At her conception, God protected her from original sin* (sin that was passed on from Adam to all humans). God also protected her from sin* throughout her life. It is taken in part from Lk. 1:28. (See also Catholicism, Roman; Theotokos.)

IMMANENCE. (From Latin: in-, in, and manere, to stay near.) The closeness or involvement of God with the world and his people. He is keeping all his creation* alive and guiding it (Ps. 136:25). He also lives in the hearts of those who love him (Isa. 57:15). It is often contrasted with the truth of God's transcendence* (he is separate from his creation). (See also Attributes of God; Transcendence.)

IMMANUEL. (From Hebrew: im, with, anu, us, and el, God.) A name for Jesus meaning, "God with us" (Isa. 7:14; Matt. 1:23). (See also Christology; Incarnation.)

IMMENSITY OF GOD. (From Latin: immensus, cannot be measured.) The belief that God is not limited by space or time. He is everywhere at the same time. He is too large to be measured. (See also Infinite, Infinity; Omnipresent.)

IMMERSION. One form of baptism.* The person is put under the water so it completely covers them and then raised out of it. There are three reasons for this form. (1) The word "baptism" means to put under water. (2) They believe this form best symbolizes the meaning of baptism (Rom. 6:3-4). (3) It was practiced by the early church. (See also Baptism; Pouring; Sprinkling.)

IMMINENCE. Something that is ready to happen very soon. The OT and NT teach that the Day of the Lord,* the time of God's judgment is imminent. As a part of that, Jesus return will be without any warning. Also, Jesus could take the church at any moment (rapture*). (See also Day of the Lord; Rapture; Second Coming of Christ.)

IMMORTALITY. (From Latin: in-, without, and mortalis, death.) The ability to live forever, not to die, not to be separate. It is a gift from God. It is used in three different ways. (1) Physical immortality is a person's body living forever. No one has this. (2) Spiritual immortality is never being separated from God. Only believers have this. (3) Immortality of the soul is the teaching that the soul,* the non-physical part of the person, is what is truly real. It will live forever and will never die. The body is just a outer covering. This third understanding is not taught in the Bible. (See also Conditional Immortality; Death; Mortality.)

IMMUTABILITY. (From Latin: in-, not, and mutare, to change.) The belief that God does not change. We can depend on God always to be the same. He is the same in his nature, desire and purpose. Jas. 1:17 and Mal. 3:6 teach this truth. This does not mean that he never acts or responds to his people. It just means that his response is consistent with his nature. It is a very important belief because it means we can depend on God. Many modern theologies, including Process Theology,* deny this. (See also Attributes of God.)

IMPASSIBILITY. (From Latin: in-, not, and pati, to

suffer.) (1) The belief that God has no emotions (i.e., love) and cannot suffer. This is the traditional explanation of impassiblity. (2) Today's understanding is that humans cannot make God suffer unless he chooses to. God is never the victim of humans. However, he chooses to suffer and feel the pain of his people. An example is at Jesus' death. Some disagree with this belief. Some misunderstand it as saying God never suffers with his people. (See also Attributes of God; Passion of Christ.)

IMPECCABILITY OF CHRIST. (Latin word: in-, not, and peccare, to sin.) The teaching that Christ was without sin.* It means both that he did not sin and that he was holy.* It is based on 2 Cor. 5:21 and Heb. 4:15 along with many other verses. There is much discussion on whether or not Christ could have sinned. Some use this to mean that Christ was not able to sin. Because he did not sin, he could be our Savior.* (See also Christology; Sin.)

IMPUTATION. (From Latin: imputare, to charge to one's account.) A legal term meaning to transfer the legal standing of a person to someone else. It is used in three ways in the Bible. (1) The guilt* of Adam's sin is transferred to all humanity (Rom. 5:12 21). (2) The guilt of all human sin is transferred to Christ (1 Pet. 2:24). (3) God transfers the righteous* standing of Christ to all believers (Rom. 5:15). Sometimes "imputed" is contrasted with "imparted" righteousness or guilt. Imparted refers to the giving of a quality or character. (See also Justification, Justify; Original Sin; Righteousness.)

INAUGURATED ESCHATOLOGY. The view that the

end time events prophesied in the OT are now both a present and future reality. Jesus started some of these events, but there are more to come. His death and resurrection* began a new stage of his kingdom.* However, there are even more stages to come. There will be very different kinds of events that will complete the end of the age.* It is "already" present, but "not yet" complete. We are in the last times, but not in the final state.* For example, believers already have been declared righteous (justification*), but not yet made completely righteous (glorification*). (See also Eschatology; Realized Eschatology.)

INCARNATION. (From Latin: in, in, and caro, flesh.) The act of the Son of God becoming a human being. It was when Christ, the Second Person of the Trinity* who was already alive, was born in Bethlehem. He did not stop being God. He also took on a full human nature (Jn. 1:14; Phil. 2:7 8.) (See also Christology; Pre-existence of Christ; Deity of Christ.)

INDULGENCES. (From Latin: indulgere, to be kind to.) In Roman Catholic* theology, the removal of the punishment of sin.* It removes the punishment that will be given in purgatory,* the place people go after death to pay for their sins. It may remove part or all of the punishment. It can only be given when the guilt has already been forgiven (absolution*). Before the Reformation (16th century), indulgences were able to be sold even before a person sinned. (See also Catholicism, Roman; Forgiveness; Sin.)

INERRANCY, BIBLICAL. (From Latin: in-, not, and errare, to wander from what is right.) The belief that the Bible is true, free from error. It is the commitment to believe as truth from God whatever the Bible actually teaches after we have studied it carefully. It is understood in many ways. For example, some say it is true only in areas of salvation.* Others say the facts of history and science are also true. An important issue is how specific the author meant to be. Another issue is the meaning of truth.* A main result of one's view of inerrancy is the amount of authority* given to the Bible. (See also Bibliology; Infallibility, Biblical; Inspiration, Bible; Revelation.)

INFALLIBILITY, BIBLICAL. (From Latin: in-, not, and fallere, to fail.) The belief that the Bible is trustworthy. It will not fail in its purpose to make us understand salvation* (2 Tim. 3:15). The authors of the Bible never try to mislead people. Throughout history, until recent years, it meant the same thing as inerrancy* (completely true, without error). Today it is often used to mean that the Bible is true only in the areas of faith and salvation. (See also Bibliology; Inerrancy; Revelation.)

INFALLIBILITY, PAPAL. (From Latin: in-, not, and fallere, to fail.) The Roman Catholic* belief that the Pope* speaks without error what the church should believe. God makes him able to do this. This applies only when he is speaking "ex cathedra,"* in his office as the leader of the church. This teaching was defined in Vatican I in 1870. (See also Catholicism, Roman; Pope.)

INFANT BAPTISM. (SEE BAPTISM, INFANT.)

INFANT SALVATION. The question of whether Christ died to save* very young children. It asks if they can be saved even though they have not heard or understood to the gospel. It especially concerns children who have died. (See also Salvation.)

INFINITE, INFINITY. (From Latin: in-, without, and finire, to end.) Without limits or end. God is infinite. Nothing can limit him. It includes areas like space, power, time, wisdom, goodness, knowledge. In contrast, humans are limited in all these areas. (See also Attributes of God; Omnipotence; Omnipresence; Omniscience.)

INFRALAPSARIANISM. (From Latin: infra, below, after, and lapsus, fall.) A Calvinistic* view of the logical order of God's decrees.* It refers to the order of the plan of God before the world began, not the order of events in history. It says God decided to let humans fall into sin* before he decided to choose some for salvation.* The order of decrees in this view is: (1) to create people; (2) to let them fall into sin; (3) to choose some people to be saved and leave others in their sin; and (4) to send Christ to save those chosen for salvation. The opposite view is supralapsarian.* (See also Decree; Supralapsarian.)

INHERITANCE. The property or position that a person gives when they die to another, usually a child. As adopted* children of God, believers share in Jesus' inheritance. (See also Adoption; Heir.)

INIQUITY. (SEE SIN.)

INSCRIPTURATION. (From Latin: in-, in, and scriptura, a writing.) The process by which God put his revelation* into writing. It was done by the inspiration* of the Holy Spirit using human authors (2 Tim. 3:16). (See also Canon; Inspiration, Bible.)

INSPIRATION, BIBLE. (From Latin: in-, in, and spirare, to breathe.) The work of the Holy Spirit* in the lives of the authors of the Bible. He prepared and moved them so that what they wrote was actually the Word of God.* The purpose was so people would know God and his way of salvation.* "Inspiration" is taken from the word meaning "God-breathed" in 2 Tim. 3:16. (See also Plenary Inspiration; Verbal Inspiration.)

INTERCESSION. (From Latin: inter, between, and cedere, to go.) To ask God to give something to another person; to pray* for someone else. It is used in two ways. (1) Christians are told to pray for other people. (2) Christ is now in heaven interceding for believers. This is a part of his ministry as our high priest.* (See also High Priest; Intercession; Work of Christ.)

INTERMEDIATE STATE. The time between a person's death and being raised from the dead at the end of time. There are many different views of what happens during this time. Most Christians believe that believers are with Christ and unbelievers are punished. (See also Eschatology.)

INTERPRETATION, BIBLICAL. (SEE HERMENEUTICS.)

INTERTESTAMENTAL. (From Latin: inter, between.) The time between the completion of the OT and the beginning of NT events. It is most often called the Intertestamental Period.

INVISIBLE CHURCH. (SEE CHURCH, INVISIBLE.)

IRRESISTIBLE GRACE. The grace of God that cannot be rejected or turned aside. It is the view that God gives a special grace to those whom he has chosen, so that chosen person always comes to faith and is saved. It is sometimes called effectual grace.* It is part of Calvinism* and is the "I" in TULIP.* (See also Effectual Grace; TULIP.)

JEHOVAH. (SEE YAHWEH.)

JESUS. (Greek form of the Hebrew name: Yeshua, Yahweh saves.) The second person of the Trinity* who lived as a man in Nazareth. He died on a cross for the sins of the world. Then he was raised from the dead. Now he lives in heaven at God's right hand. His name was given by the angel* of God (Lk. 1:31) and means "Yahweh* saves." (See also Christology; Logos; Messiah; Resurrection of Christ; Virgin Birth.)

JEW. A person who is either born in the Hebrew race or who practices the religion of Israel (or both). Many people today who disagree over exactly who should be called a Jew. (See also Judaism.)

JOY. A pleasure or delight that is deep within a person. It cannot be lessened by the troubles of life. It is one of the fruits of the Spirit* (Gal. 5:22). God gives joy. (See also Fruit of the Spirit; Hope.)

JUDAISM. The religion and culture of the people of Israel, the Jews.* (See also Jew; Pharisees; Sadducees.)

JUDAIZE. (From Greek: Ioudaizo, to follow Jewish customs.) A NT term meaning to make a Gentile* (non Jew) follow Jewish customs and laws so they could be a Christian. There were some Christians in the early church who made Gentiles follow the law of Moses and other Jewish customs. Paul criticized Peter because he did this (Gal. 2:14). The message of Galatians is that judaizing is wrong. (See also Gentile; Jew; Mosaic Law.)

JUDGE. The person who decides whether someone or some action is good or bad. This person helps people settle disagreements. (1) God is judge over everything (Gen. 18:25). (2) In the OT, after the Exodus there were judges who ruled the land. (3) Also, Jesus is the judge of all people (Acts 10:42). (See also Judgment.)

JUDGMENT. The decision about whether a person is good or bad. Usually it means condemnation,* the decision that the person is guilty.* In the Bible, God, the judge, makes decisions based on his perfect law. Some of his judgment happens today as a result of sin (i.e., the flood, Israel in captivity). Some will happen at the end of the ages,* when he will judge all people and sin will be punished. (See also Condemn, Condemnation; Judgment

Seat; Last Judgment.)

JUDGMENT SEAT. The name for the judge's seat during a trial. In theology it refers to the time when Christ will judge all people at the end of time. Also called the "bema seat" which is the Greek name for the judge's seat. (See also Eschatology; Judgment; Last Judgment.)

JUST, JUSTICE. The fair treatment of others according to good laws. It often means the same thing as righteous. It is used of both God and humans. (1) God is completely just because he rules his kingdom* according to his perfect character. He does not favor some people over others. (2) He commands humans to live by those rules also (Amos 5:24). It is also used for proper relationships in social life. (See also Attributes of God; Righteousness; Social Gospel.)

JUSTIFICATION, JUSTIFY. To declare, accept and treat a person as just* or righteous.* That person is no longer to be treated as guilty,* but as innocent. It is a legal, not a moral term. At conversion,* God has removed the guilt of sin that was against believers. He has now said that they are not guilty. This is because Christ paid the penalty for sin. Believers were also given his righteousness. They are also brought back into relationship with God. (See also Adoption; Faith; Reconciliation; Righteousness; Salvation; Sanctification.)

KENOSIS, KENOTIC THEOLOGY. (Greek word: kenosis, to empty.) A word used in Phil. 2:7 which says "Christ emptied himself." There have been many views of

* Defined elsewhere in Dictionary

what he emptied himself of. It is especially used of theologies that teach Jesus gave up part of his nature as God. (See also Christology; Hypostatic Union.)

KERYGMA. (Greek word: kerygma, the message preached.) In the Bible, it refers to the message of the gospel* or the preaching itself. In theology, it means the content of the message Jesus preached. (See also Gospel.)

KESWICK. The name of a place in northern England where there is a gathering of Christians. There are now many of these gatherings throughout the world. They gather to commit themselves to holiness.* It is used in theology to describe a view of how Christians become holy. It focuses on our union with Christ.* It teaches that we must stop working hard to become holy, but just let the Holy Spirit control us. (See also Holy, Holiness; Sanctification.)

KINGDOM OF GOD, CHRIST, HEAVEN. The active rule of God over his creation.* He establishes it by redeeming* it from evil, judging the enemies, and giving his blessing.* He does that for and through his people. All is done for God's own glory.* "Kingdom of Christ" em-phasizes the Messiah's* part in the kingdom work. "Kingdom of Heaven" is Matthew's term for Kingdom of God. (See also Eschatology.)

KOINONIA. (SEE FELLOWSHIP.)

LAITY. (From Greek: laos, people.) (1) In the Bible it is the whole people of God (1 Pet. 2:9 10). (2) In the church today it is used for the people in a church who are not set apart (ordained*) for specific ministry. Those other people are the "clergy."* (See also Clergy.)

LAKE OF FIRE. The place where the wicked will be punished forever. It is used six times in the book of Revelation. A term meaning the same thing is "second death."* (See also Death, The Second; Hell; Judgment.)

LAMB OF GOD. A name John the Baptist called Jesus (Jn. 1:29, 35). Jesus would take away the sins* of the world. People disagree over whether he was referring to the lamb of sacrifice* or of the lamb of Passover.* (See also Christology; Passover.)

LAST DAY(S). The time at the end of the age.* The focus of the OT description of it is a time when God will judge evil and save his people. The focus of the NT description is the time when Jesus will return. There is a difference between the last days and the last day. The last days has already begun. It started with ministry of Jesus (Heb. 1:2). In contrast, the last day is still future. It is the Day of the Lord,* when Jesus will return to judge the world and bring everything to its final purpose. It is also sometimes called last times. (See also Inaugurated Eschatology; Day of the Lord; Eschatology; Judgment; Second Coming of Christ.)

LAST JUDGMENT. The judgment that will happen at the end of the age.* Christ will judge all people and nations at that time. He will punish unbelievers for sin and reward believers for good works. It is a part of the

"Day of the Lord."* (See also Day of the Lord; Judgment.)

LAST SUPPER. (SEE LORD'S SUPPER.)

LAST TIMES. (SEE LAST DAY(S).)

LAW. Rules, commandments, orders to be obeyed. (1) Most broadly, it is the whole set of rules God has given to help people know and love him and live with other people. (2) The first five books of the OT, the Torah is called the "law." (3) The Mosaic Law* is the OT law of Moses, the old covenant. This is the usual meaning when the Bible capitalizes "Law." (See also Mosaic Law.)

LAYING ON OF HANDS. The practice of touching a person as a point of identification. Sometimes it has the idea of giving them something (i.e., blessing,* power, authority,* etc.) It was used in the OT with an animal sacrifice* and for blessing (Lev. 16:21; Gen. 48). It was used in the NT to heal and set apart for ministry* (Acts 28:8; 1 Tim. 4:14). (See also Bless; Ordain, Ordination; Sacrifice.)

LEGALISM. The view that life is to be focused on obeying the law.* It is especially used of the belief or practice that says we earn God's favor by obeying the law, rather than just by grace.* We do what is pleasing to God by following laws rather than developing Christian character. It especially centers on OT law. (See also Antinomian; Law; Pharisees.)

LIBERALISM, THEOLOGICAL. A theological movement which is willing to change some of the commonly accepted (orthodox*) teachings of Christianity. (1) "Classical Liberalism" was a movement in the 19th and early 20th centuries. They taught several truths: (a) "The Fatherhood of God" -- God is our Father; (b) "The brotherhood of man" -- all humans are related to each other; (c) "The ethic of love" -- our greatest responsibility is to love everyone; and (d) "The great value of every human soul." (2) Today liberalism comes in many different forms. There are several teachings which would be true about most theological liberalism. (a) The gospel must be adapted to today's world view.* (b) The Bible is a book of religious experience, not God's revelation* of himself. Biblical criticism* is a regular practice. (c) The supernatural* world of miracles* is not real. (d) We can know God within ourself or the world. It says the Bible is not revelation. (e) Humans are very good. They are not born sinful* and guilty.* It is also called modernism. Its opposite is evangelicalism* or fundamental-ism.* (See also Criticism, Higher; Evangelical, Evangelicalism; Fundamentalism; Orthodox, Orthodoxy.)

LIBERATION THEOLOGY. A group of theologies that say the main goal of the church is to free people who are oppressed. It seeks to free those who are forced to obey by the wrong use of power. Salvation* means freeing from sin.* However, sin is not defined as guilt* before God. Sin is defined as suffering in economic, political and social ways. Some examples are Third World, Black and Feminist Theologies. (See also Salvation; Sin.)

LIGHT. (1) Literally, something that gives brightness. (2) Often it is a word picture used in the Bible to describe God and Jesus (1 Jn. 1:5; Jn. 8:12). (3) Light is also used to mean good and darkness to mean evil.

LIMITED ATONEMENT. (SEE ATONEMENT, LIMITED.)

LITERALISM. The translation or interpretation of the Bible which uses the most exact meaning of words. It is a commitment to take the most plain, normal, clear ordinary sense that the whole context requires. It tries to find exactly what the author meant. The opposite is the allegor-ical* method which tries to find a deeper, hidden meaning behind the words. (See also Allegorical Method, Allegorizing; Hermeneutics.)

LOGOS. (Greek word: logos, word, speech, reason.) A title for Christ, the Second Person of the Trinity* (Jn. 1:1, 14). It is used to show that he is God's communication to humans. The idea probably came from both the Greek world and the OT understanding of God speaking his word.* It is used often in the writings of the early church. (See also Christology; Jesus; Word, Word of God, Word of the Lord.)

LORD. A title for God and Jesus. In the OT it is the translation for Yahweh* and Adonai*. In the NT, it is the name for Jesus. It means ruler, leader, the one who is in charge. When the NT calls Jesus "Lord," it is saying he is God, just like Yahweh in the OT (Rom. 10:9). When "Lord" is used to translate Yahweh in English Bibles it is often put in all capitalized letters (i.e., LORD). That way it is different from the translation of Adonai which is Lord. (See also Adonai; Christology; Deity of Christ; Jesus; Trinity; Yahweh.)

LORD'S PRAYER. The model prayer* Jesus gave in Matt. 6:9 13. Sometimes it is used for Jesus' prayer in Jn. 17. (See also Prayer.)

LORD'S SUPPER. The sacrament* or ordinance* of eating bread and drinking wine (or grape juice). On Passover,* the night before Jesus' death, he did it with his disciples* and told them to do it regularly. Jesus said it is a way we remember his death and look forward to his return. It is sometimes called the Eucharist which is the Greek word meaning "to give thanks." It is also called Communion. Some people make a distinction between the "Last Supper" and "Lord's Supper." The "Last Supper" was the actual night when Jesus began the practice. The "Lord's Supper" is the times when we remember it. There are many different interpretations of it. (See also Dynamic Presence; Memorialism; Real Presence; Transubstantiation.)

LORDSHIP SALVATION. The name of a debate about faith* among Christians today. (1) Part of the question is the nature of saving faith. One side says a person must just believe in Jesus as Savior.* The other side says a commitment to follow Jesus as Lord* is also necessary to be saved. (2) Coming out of this, the other part of the question is the basis of how we can know if we are saved (assurance*). The first side says we can be sure of our salvation* based on our belief in Christ. The other side says the good works* coming out of our faith make us sure of our salvation. (See also Assurance; Faith; Salvation.)

LOVE. Seeking the best for another person. It is used in many different ways in the Bible. (1) It is one of God's qualities (attributes*). 1 Jn. 4:8 says God is love. Some theologians see it as the most important attribute of God. (2) It is a command to believers. Jesus said loving God is the greatest commandment and loving others is second (Mk. 12:29 31). It is the way others will know that we love God (Jn. 13:35). (See also Attributes of God.)

LUCIFER. (SEE SATAN.)

LUTHERANISM. A system of theology* started by Martin Luther (1483-1546) a German Reformer. The main distinctives from Roman Catholicism* (as with all Protestant* theologies) can be summed up in four "solas." (1) Sola Scriptura -- the Bible* is the only authority* for Christian truth. (2) Sola gratia -- we are saved by grace* only and not by anything we do. (3) Sola fide -- faith* is the only way to be saved. (4) Sola Christus -- Christ's work on the cross is the only means by which a person is saved. A main difference from Reformed theology* is the view of the Lord's Supper.* Lutherans believe in "real presence,"* the body and blood of Christ are actually "in, with, and under" the bread and wine. Christ is also "in, with, and under" the water in baptism.* (See also Calvinism; Catholicism, Roman; Protestantism; Real Presence.)

LXX. (SEE SEPTUAGINT.)

MAN. (1) Human beings, the highest of God's creation* (Gen. 1:26). It often refers to both males and females. But it is also used for just males. (2) In the NT, Paul uses "one new man" to speak of all the people of God as a unity* (Eph. 2:14-16). (3) The part of theology that deals with humans is called anthropology.* (See also Anthropology; Image of God, Imago Dei; Man, Old and New.)

MAN, OLD AND NEW. Terms used by Paul to speak about the difference between life without and with Christ. The old man is the person who is united* with Adam and separated from Christ (Rom. 5:12-6:14). The new man is the person who is united with Christ.* The main places the terms are used are Rom. 6:6; Eph. 4:22 24; Col. 3:9 10. (See also Nature, Old and New; Union with Christ.)

MARRIAGE FEAST/SUPPER OF THE LAMB. An end time event mentioned in Rev. 19:7 9. It is the time when the church, the bride,* will be joined with Christ. (See also Bride, Bridegroom; Eschatology.)

MEANS OF GRACE. The way or channel in which God gives grace to people. It is usually used with baptism* and the Lord's Supper.* It is also sometimes used with preaching, prayer* and other Christian practices. (See also Ordinance; Sacraments.)

MEDIATION, MEDIATOR. (From Latin: medius, middle.) The person who works between two people or groups to help them be friends. It is especially used between God and humans. In the OT, the prophet* and priest* were the mediators who worked to bring God and humans into relationship with each other. In the NT, Jesus is the mediator. Because of his death as a punishment for sin, humans can be at peace with God and each other (1 Tim. 2:3 6). (See also Reconciliation; Savior.)

MEMORIALISM. The view of the Lord's Supper* started by Ulrich Zwingli (1484-1531), a Swiss Reformer. It teaches that the bread and wine are just symbols* to remind us of Christ's death. Christ is not any more present than at any other time. It opposed both the Catholic* and Lutheran* views. (See also Dynamic Presence; Lord's Supper; Real Presence; Transubstantiation.)

MERCY. Giving someone more than or different from what they deserve. It is one of the qualities (attributes*) of God (Isa. 63:7). He shows mercy when he forgives* our sin. Believers are also commanded to show mercy to other people (Jas. 2:13). (See also Attributes of God; Grace.)

MERCY SEAT. The gold cover of the ark of the covenant.* It was in the Holy of Holies,* the center room of the tabernacle* or temple.* It became the symbol* for God's forgiveness* of sins. That was because, on the Day of Atonement,* the blood was sprinkled on it. (See also Ark of the Covenant; Day of Atonement; Forgiveness.)

MESSIAH. (From Hebrew: mashiah, to anoint, smear with oil.) The leader promised by God in the OT. He would come to carry out God's plan of salvation.* The NT says Jesus is the Messiah. "Christ"* is the Greek word for Messiah. (See also Christ; Christology; Jesus.)

METAPHYSICS. (From Greek: meta, after, and physic, the [books of] nature.) The part of philosophy* that deals with what is truly real. It tries to describe the true nature of life, God, etc. It is sometimes called ontology. (See also Philosophy.)

MIDTRIBULATION. One of the views about the rapture,* the time God will take the church out of the world. It is the view that the church will go through the first half (usually 3 1/2 years) of the tribulation.* God will protect the church during that time. Then it will be taken up to be with Christ. During the last half the suffering and trouble on earth will get much worse. (See also Eschatology; Great Tribulation; Postribulation; Pretribulation; Rapture; Tribulation.)

MILLENNIUM. (From Latin: mille, thousand, and annus, year.) The personal kingly rule of Christ on the earth. It literally means 1000 years. Some say the Bible is teaching it will last 1000 years, but others believe it refers to just a long period of time. It is taken from Rev. 20:1 10. Some believe OT prophecy also speaks of it (Isa. 2, 11; Zech. 14). It will be a time of peace, goodness, justice, and riches. There are many views of how long, when and where it will be. It is sometimes called "Chiliasm" from the Greek word, chilias, meaning a thousand. (See also Amillennialism; Eschatology; Premillennialism; Postmillennialism; Second Coming of Christ.)

MINISTER, MINISTRY. (From Latin: minister, a servant.) Service to God and people. Used in a broad sense, it is done by all believers as a result of faith. Used in a narrow sense, it describes those who are set aside by the church in an official way. (See also Clergy; Offices, Church; Pastoral Theology.)

MIRACLE. (From Latin: miraculum, wonder.) God working in the world in a special way that is different from the normal laws of creation.* It is done to show the power of God. The Bible also calls it a "sign" to show that it points to God and his saving work. Today many non-evangelicals* question if miracles really happened. However, the resur-rection of Christ* is the greatest miracle and is the basis of the Christian faith. (See also Resurrection of Christ; Spiritual Gifts; Supernatural; Virgin Birth.)

MISSION, MISSIONS, MISSIOLOGY. (From Latin: missio, a sending away.) The responsibility of the church to take the gospel* to the whole world. It is especially used of taking it to another culture.* Missiology is the study of missions. (See also Contextualization; Evangelism; Gospel.)

MODALISM. The error that teaches that the Trinity* is just three revelations of the one God. It says that the Father, Son, and Spirit are not three separate persons in one God. They are three names, modes, ways of working, or roles of the one God. (See also Monarchianism; Trinity.)

MODERNISM. (SEE LIBERALISM, THEOLOGICAL.)

MONARCHIANISM. (From Greek: monos, only and arche, ruler.) The belief in the oneness or unity* of God. It was developed in the third century to emphasize the sole rule of the one God and guard against the belief in three gods (tritheism*). It led to the error of denying that there are three persons in the one God. One type is modalistic* -- the one God appears in three different forms. The other type is adoptionistic* -- God "adopted" a merely human Jesus and gave him a divine* spirit at his baptism. (See also Adoptionism; Modalism; Trinity; Tritheism.)

MONERGISM. (From Greek: monos, one, and ergo, to work.) The belief that it is only God's grace* that converts a person. God begins and completes salvation.* Humans are unable to save themselves. It is taught by Augustinianism.* The opposite view is synergism* (the work of God and humans together saves a person). (See also Augustinian-ism; Salvation; Synergism.)

MONISM. (From Greek: monos, one, only.) A view in philosophy* that says there is only one reality. The world of ideas or the physical world are the most common ways of understanding this reality. In religious monism, both God and the world are parts of one large whole. It is a part of Hinduism, Buddhism, scientific materialism, and other religions and philosophies. (See also Dualism; Philosophy.)

MONOPHYSITISM. (From Greek: monos, one, single, and physis, nature.) A teaching about Christ that says he has only one nature. He is only God, not human. He just has a human body. It is sometimes called Eutychianism after Eutyches (c. 378-454) of Constantinople. This view is not accepted by orthodox* Christians today. (See also Christology; Hypostatic Union.)

MONOTHEISM. (From Greek: mono, one, and theos, God.) The belief that there is only one God. It is often used for Israel's belief in one God as opposed to the other religions which had many gods. Christianity, Judaism and Islam are the three main monotheistic religions. (See also Polytheism; Theism.)

MORAL ARGUMENT. The attempt to prove there is a God because there are similar moral values in different nations. It says that there is a God because people from different cultures have the same basic morals. Therefore, there must be someone who gave those morals. (See also Anthropological Arguments; Theistic Proofs.)

MORAL EVIL. A kind of evil* which is the bad things that come from human actions and hurts people. Examples are killing another person or lying. The other kind is natural evil,* the bad things that happen in creation* (i.e., floods, earthquakes.) (See Evil; Natural Evil.)

MORAL INABILITY. (SEE SPIRITUAL INABILITY.)

MORAL INFLUENCE THEORY. (SEE ATONEMENT, MORAL INFLUENCE.)

MORAL THEOLOGY. The Roman Catholic* study of good and evil, right and wrong. It is another term for what Protestants* call Christian ethics. In Roman Catholic theology, it is especially used in relation to the sacrament of penance.* (See also Catholicism, Roman; Ethics; Penance.)

MORALITY. (From Latin: moralis, manner, custom, actions.) The basis by which we decide whether our actions are right or wrong, good or evil. The principles or rules which guide our life. (See also Ethics.)

MORTAL. (From Latin: mortalis, death.) The fact that someone is able to and will die. In theology it speaks of physical death.* But the believer will live after physical death. (See also Death; Immortality.)

MORTAL SIN. (SEE SIN, MORTAL.)

MOSAIC LAW. The group of rules which God gave to Moses. It is often used for the whole Old Covenant, the rules for the relationship between God and Israel. (See also Law; New Covenant.)

MOTHER OF GOD. (SEE THEOTOKOS.)

MYSTERY. (From Greek: mysterion, a secret of God.) Something that is unknown, hidden or not completely understood. Paul uses it to refer to that which was hidden, but has now been revealed. He uses it most often for the gospel* (1 Cor. 2:7; Col. 2:2). He also uses it for the fact that now Jews* and Gentiles* come before God equally

(Eph. 3:6). (See also Gospel; Revelation.)

MYSTICISM. (From Greek: mystikos, part of God's secrets.) A type of religion that seeks and focuses on a personal experience of God. Mystics try to know him directly in a loving way. They even try to be united with God. They do not want just to know through other people or just know about him. (See also Identification with Christ; Union with Christ.)

MYTH. (From Greek: mythos, a story, word, speech.) Generally, an untrue story that expresses the religious insights and cultural* values of a people. It is designed to symbolize* or explain the mysteries of human experience. It is used in more specific ways in theology. It is especially used by Bultmann (1884-1976) of Germany in his method of demythol-ogization.* He believes the Bible tells the gospel in mythical, not historical, stories which reflect an ancient world view. We must free the gospel from these myths. Bultmann says the true meaning is complete dependence upon God. (See also Demythologization; Neo-Orthodoxy.)

NAME. What a person was called was very important in Bible times. A name described a person or told you something about them. Giving a name showed your rule over them (2 Sam. 12:28). (See also Adonai; Jesus; Yahweh.)

NATURAL EVIL. A kind of evil which is the bad things that come from creation,* apart from human actions. Examples are earthquakes or floods. The other kind is moral evil,* the bad things that happen because of human action (i.e., lying, killing.) (See Evil; Moral Evil.)

NATURAL LAW. (1) In theology, it usually refers to the sense of right and wrong that is in every person's heart. It is knowing what is good and evil by our consciences or by looking at the world. We do not need God's law* to tell us what is good or evil. For example, even people who have not heard God's law know that murder is wrong. Rom. 2:14 15 speaks of natural law. (2) It is also used for the rules of science. The law of gravity is an example of this type. (See also Con-science; Ethics; Morality.)

NATURAL REVELATION. (SEE REVELATION, NATURAL.)

NATURAL THEOLOGY. Truth that can be known about God from the created things and reason alone. It is the belief that God can be known apart from Him revealing* himself. Theistic proofs* are a part of it. It is humans reaching to God in contrast to God's revelation to us in grace. (See also Revelation, General; Theistic Proofs.)

NATURALISM. The belief that this world is all there really is. There is no God, no spiritual beings (angels*), and no life after death. Super-naturalism* is the opposite view, which is the Christian view. (See also Supernatural.)

NATURE, OLD AND NEW. These terms are only used in theology, not in the Bible. Generally, the old nature is the sinful nature of a person. It is the desire to be apart from God and do wrong. The new nature is the spiritual nature of a person. It is the new heart which is given by the Holy Spirit. These terms are often used the same as "Old Man"* and "New Man."* (See also Flesh, Fleshly; Man, Old and New; Regenera-tion.)

NECESSARY BEING. A term in philosophy* for the one that must exist or have life by its very nature. It is the cause of all. In theology, God is seen to be the necessary being. He does not depend on anyone else for life. He has life in himself. He must live. He is unable not to exist. In contrast, all other creatures are "contingent beings." Everything else also depends on him so it can exist or live. We need God so we can live (Acts 17:28). (See also Aseity; Essence; Philosophy.)

NEO PENTECOSTALISM. (SEE CHARISMATIC MOVEMENT.)

NEO-EVANGELICALISM. A movement that started in the United States about 1947. It agreed with most of the evangelical* teachings. It was different because it emphasized more intellectual thought and more application to social problems. Some evangelical beliefs have been changed a little. For example, not all neo evangelicals would believe the Bible is without error. Sometimes it is called "new evangelicalism." It is a negative term used by fundamentalists* for those whom they believe have compromised the gospel to be relevant to secular* society. (See also Evangelicalism; Fundamentalism.)

NEO-ORTHODOXY. (From Greek: neos, new, ortho, right, straight, and dokein, to think.) The "new" (early 20th century) movement back toward "orthodoxy,"* commonly accepted truth. Historically, it is a group of theologies that went back close to traditional beliefs, yet was still new. It was in reaction to the liberal theology* of the 19th century. It was "new" because it accepted biblical criticism* and some existentialism* (we meet with God in person, not just in the truths of Scripture). But it was "orthodox"* because it taught human sin and God's transcendence* or separateness from his creation.* It is mostly associated with Karl Barth (1886-1968) and Emil Brunner (1889-1966), two Swiss theologians. (See also Criticism, Biblical; Demythologization; Existential, Existentialism; Orthodox, Orthodoxy.)

NESTORIANISM. A view of Christ started in the fifth century by Nestorius of Constantinople. It teaches that Christ was two separate persons, one God and one human. Both lived in the one body of Jesus. This view is not accepted by orthodox* Christians today. (See also Christology; Hypostatic Union.)

NEW BIRTH. (SEE BORN AGAIN.)

NEW COVENANT. A new relationship between God and his people which was promised in the OT for the last days.* It is the heart of the message of the NT. Jer. 31:31 37 is the main OT passage which teaches about it. God would write his law on their hearts and all would know and love God. Also, Israel would be restored. It is in contrast to the old covenant, the one with Israel through

Moses. In the NT, the new covenant is referred to in 1 Cor. 11:25 and Heb. 8:8 among others. There is much discussion on its exact nature. (See also Covenant; Promise.)

NEW CREATION, NEW CREATURE. A term used for believers after God has given them new spiritual life (regeneration*). It is used in 2 Cor. 5:17 and Gal. 6:15. (See also Man, Old and New; Regeneration.)

NEW HEAVENS AND NEW EARTH. The world after God creates it again at the end of the age.* God will be present with his people. They will worship* and serve him. It will be a place of complete righteousness.* People disagree on whether God will just renew the present heavens and earth or will create something brand new. Rom. 8:18 21; 2 Pet. 3:13; and Rev. 21:1 8 are the main passages where it is mentioned. (See also Eschatology; Heaven; Kingdom of God, Christ, Heaven.)

NEW MAN. (SEE MAN, OLD AND NEW.)

NEW NATURE. (SEE NATURE, OLD AND NEW.)

NIHILISM. (From Latin: nihil, nothing.) The view that denies any objective basis for truth,* especially moral truth. Therefore, it rejects all authority,* tradition* and morality.* It is the view that everything that was once believed to be true or good should be rejected. That includes God and all religion and many other things. (See also Atheism; Philosophy.)

OBEDIENCE, OBEY. To do what you are told to do. The Bible tells us that obeying God is a result of loving him (Jn. 14:15). Christ is our example of obedience (Phil. 2:8). (See also Sanctification.)

OCCULT, OCCULTISM. (From Latin: occultus, hidden, covered.) Literally, hidden or secret wisdom. It is a practice of seeking contact with evil spirits. It looks for experience or power beyond what is normal through those contacts. It is closely connected with spiritism.* The Bible clearly teaches occultism is evil (Deut. 18:10 11; Acts 19:19). (See also Spiritism.)

OFFICES, CHURCH. A position of responsibility and authority.* The people are chosen and given authority to do the job. The office is separate from the person filling it and lasts beyond the person. Elders* and deacons* are two biblical offices. There are often many other offices in a church. (See also Deacon, Deaconess; Elder.)

OFFICES OF CHRIST. The roles or functions of Christ. Three are usually listed as the main ones. (1) Christ is prophet.* He brings the Father's message of salvation* to the people and tells about the future. (2) Christ is priest.* He offered a sacrifice and now prays for believers. (3) He is also king. He rules his kingdom* and will conquer his enemies. (See also Christology; High Priest; Prophet, Prophecy.)

OLD MAN. (SEE MAN, OLD AND NEW.)

OLD NATURE. (SEE NATURE, OLD AND NEW.)

OMNIPOTENCE. (From Latin: omnis, all, and potens, powerful.) The belief that God is all powerful. He is able to do anything that is a proper use of power. He uses his power according to his other qualities or attributes.* Ps. 115:3 and Gen. 17:1 teach this. (See also Attributes of God.)

OMNIPRESENCE. (From Latin: omnis, all, and praesens, present.) The belief that God is everywhere present at the same time. He is not limited by space. Ps. 139:7 12 teaches this truth. He does not have a body, so he is not in just one place at a time. He is at work everywhere. This is sometimes also called ubiquity. (See also Attributes of God; Immensity.)

OMNISCIENCE. (From Latin: omnis, all, and sciens, knowing.) The belief that God knows everything. His knowledge cannot be measured. Ps. 147:5 and 1 Jn. 3:20 teach this truth. He knows the good and the bad. Nothing can be hidden from him (Ps. 139:7-12). He knows the past, present, and the future. (See also Attributes of God; Wisdom.)

ONLY BEGOTTEN. The common translation of the Greek word mono-genes (Jn. 3:16). It is used for Jesus to show that he has a special relationship with God the Father that no one else has. Traditionally it was understood to refer to the fathering of the Son, both eternally (eternal generation*) and in the incarnation* and virgin birth* of Jesus. God was the father of Jesus. Had no human father. More recently many scholars have come to believe that the real meaning is "one of a kind" or "only one." (See also

Christology; Eternal Generation; Trinity.)

ONTOLOGICAL ARGUMENT. (From Greek: onta, being, true reality.) The attempt of Anselm (c. 1033-1109) of Italy to prove there is a God. The argument is: (1) God is "that than which nothing greater can be conceived" (thought of). By definition God could not be less than the greatest object of our knowledge; (2) That which exists in reality is greater than that which exists only in thinking; (3) Therefore, God must exist in reality as well as in thinking or there would be something greater than God. The proof draws on the knowledge of himself God places in the minds of all human beings (Rom. 1:18ff). It is based on thinking alone, not on what we see in the world. (See also Theistic Proofs.)

ONTOLOGY. (SEE METAPHYSICS.)

OPEN THEISM. A new perspective on God emphasizing (from Greek: onta, being, true reality.) The attempt of Anselm (c. 1033-1109) of Italy to prove there is a God. The argument is: (1) God is "that than which nothing greater can be conceived" (thought of). By definition God could not be less than the greatest object of our knowledge; (2) That which exists in reality is greater than that which exists only in thinking; (3) Therefore, God must exist in reality as well as in thinking or there would be something greater than God. The proof draws on the knowledge of himself God places in the minds of all human beings (Rom. 1:18ff). It is based on thinking alone, not on what we see in the world. (See also Theistic Proofs.) A modern form of Socinianism associated with

Clark Pinnock, John Sanders

ORDAIN, ORDINATION. (From Latin: ordo, to set in order.) To set apart a person for a certain ministry* or office.* Biblical examples are Jer. 1:5; Mk. 3:14; Tit. 1:5. Some believe that it gives a person a special power for ministry. Others say it is just recognizing the spiritual gifts* God has already given. "Ordain" is also used in the Bible to speak of God planning what will happen in the future. (See also Clergy; Decree; Laying on of Hands; Minister, Ministry; Offices, Church; Predestination.)

ORDINANCE. (From Latin: ordo, to set in order.) A practice commanded by Jesus to be done regularly by the church. An ordinance is a symbol* that reminds us of certain truths. Baptism* and the Lord's Supper* are the two ordinances in Protestant* churches. The term is used instead of "sacrament"* because of the belief that God does not give grace through them. (See also Baptism; Lord's Supper; Means of Grace; Sacrament; Symbol.)

ORDER OF SALVATION, ORDO SALUTIS. The logical ordering of the different parts of salvation.* It is the attempt to decide what parts come before or after other parts. For example, people are saved before they are made holy* (sanctification*). (See also Salvation.)

ORIGINAL RIGHTEOUSNESS. The moral goodness of Adam and Eve before they sinned. Gen. 1:31 says God's creation was "very good." It was lost after humans sinned. (See also Image of God, Imago Dei; Righteousness.)

ORIGINAL SIN. The teaching that everyone is born guilty* and separated from God. Because Adam sinned, all humans are born sinners (Rom. 5:12-21). This results in a desire to sin. (See also Sin.)

ORTHODOX, ORTHODOXY. (From Greek: orthos, right, straight, and dokein, to think.) Literally, true or right belief. It is the opposite of heresy* or heterodoxy (hetero, other, different). It can be used in many different ways. (1) It is the official teachings of a church or group. (2) It often means that which is commonly accepted as true or right. There are several orthodox truths which have been held through history. (a) Every person needs to be saved. Salvation* comes only through Christ's substitutionary* death on the cross* to pay for our sin. That is a result of God's grace* alone. People receive it through faith.* (b) The Bible is the Word of God* and completely truthful. It is the highest authority* in a believer's life. It is higher than the church, reason, or anything else. (c) There are three persons in the one God (Trinity*). Therefore, both Jesus and the Holy Spirit are God. (d) Also, Jesus was born of a virgin,* died on a cross for human sin* and bodily rose from the dead. He will return bodily and personally to judge* all humanity at the end of the age.* (e) The miracles* of the Bible are also true. (3) It also refers to the Eastern Orthodox Church,* the part of the church which separated from the Western Church in 1054. (See also Heresy, Orthodox Church; Schism.)

ORTHODOX CHURCH. The churches* whose earthly leader is in Constantinople. It is sometimes called the

Eastern Orthodox Church. They are distinct from the Roman Catholic* and Protestant* Churches in a few ways. (1) Their theology is based on the teaching (creeds*) of the seven ecumenical* councils of the fourth to eighth centuries. They want to keep the faith of the ancient leaders of the church. This teaching of the church (tradition*) has the same authority* as the Bible. (2) They believe their teaching bishops* have the authority passed on from the apostle Peter. In this they reject the Roman Catholic belief that only the bishop of Rome (Pope*) has that authority. (3) They reject filioque,* the teaching that the Holy Spirit came from the Father "and the Son." In 1054 they split off from the Roman Church over this teaching. (See also Apostolic Succession; Catholicism, Roman; Creed; Protestantism; Tradition.)

PAEDOBAPTISM. (SEE INFANT BAPTISM.)

PAGANISM. (1) In general, religions which are animistic,* polytheistic,* or people who are not religious at all. (2) Specifically, it is used for all religions which are not Jewish, Christian or Islamic. (See also Animism; Polytheism.)

PANENTHEISM. (From Greek: pan, all, en, in, and theos, God.) The belief that everything is in God, but God is more than that. It is a part of Process Theology.* It is the attempt to give middle ground between pantheism* (all is God) and deism* (God is totally separate from the world). (See also Pantheism; Process Theology.)

PANTHEISM. (From Greek: pan, all, and theos, God.)

The belief that everything is God. All parts of the world make up God. God is nothing more than all the parts together. (See also Panentheism; Theism.)

PAPACY. (SEE POPE.)

PAPAL INFALLIBILITY. (SEE INFALLIBILITY, PAPAL.)

PARACLETE. (Greek word: para, beside, and kaleo, to call.) Literally, "the one who is called beside." It is someone who supports, encourages, comforts, counsels, or gives help. It is also a legal term for someone who speaks for or defends another person. Both Jesus (I Jn. 2:1) and the Holy Spirit (Jn. 16:6-8) are called Paraclete. "Advocate" and "Comforter" mean the same thing. (See also Holy Spirit; Jesus.)

PARADISE. (From Greek: paradeisos, park, garden.) A place of great blessing* and peace. It is used in the Bible for the garden of Eden, heaven,* and the place where God is. (See also Bless; Heaven.)

PARADOX. (From Greek: para, contrary to, and doxa, belief, opinion.) Two truths or statements which seem to contradict each other. It also may be a statement which seems to be the opposite of what is commonly believed to be true. Examples of Christian paradoxes are the God is in control of the world and yet humans freely make their own choices. Another example is the fact that Jesus is both God and human. (See also Antinomy.)

PAROUSIA. (Greek word: parousia, coming, presence.) The second coming of Christ.* Jesus, who left earth to go to be with his Father, will return to earth. (See also Advent; Second Coming of Christ.)

PASSION OF CHRIST. (From Latin: passio, suffering.) The sufferings of Jesus. It especially means Jesus' death on the cross. (See also Cross; Crucifixion; Impassibility.)

PASSOVER. The first event of the Exodus (Exod. 12). God commanded the Jews to put the blood of a lamb on their doorposts. Then the angel* of death killed all the firstborn sons of Egypt, but passed over the houses with blood on the door. God freed them from Egypt at that time. Israel remembered God's salvation of them by celebrating the feast every year. Christ is also called our Passover lamb (I Cor. 5:7). (See also Lamb of God.)

PASTORAL THEOLOGY. (From Latin: pastor, shepherd.) The part of theology* that relates to the work of the ministry.* It is the doctrinal teaching that gives the basis for ministry. It helps determine the nature of ministry. (See also Minister, Ministry.)

PELAGIANISM. The theology of Pelagius, a teacher at Rome, started in the fourth century. It emphasizes human ability. It teaches that humans are able to do enough good to save themselves without God's help. They say Adam's sin did not affect all people except to give them a bad example. The opposite is Augustinianism.* (See also Augus-tinianism; Semi-Pelagianism; Total Inability.)

PENAL SUBSTITUTION THEORY OF THE ATONEMENT. (SEE ATONEMENT, PENAL SUBSTITUTION THEORY.)

PENANCE. (From Latin: poena, penalty.) The discipline* given by the church to a member who has admitted (confessed*) their sin.* The person also must do some action so their sins will be forgiven.* It is for sins done after baptism.* It is a sacrament in the Roman Catholic* and Eastern Orthodox* churches. (See also Catholicism, Roman; Confess, Confession; Orthodox Church; Repentance; Sacrament.)

PENITENCE. (SEE REPENTANCE.)

PENTATEUCH. (From Greek: penta, five and teuchos, books.) The first five books of the OT. It is also sometimes called the "Torah." (See also Mosaic Law.)

PENTECOST. (From Greek: pentekoste, fiftieth.) A feast that comes 50 days after Passover.* In the OT, it was a time to be thankful for the grain harvest (Exod. 34:22). It is also called the feast of weeks. At the first Pentecost after Jesus's resurrection,* the Holy Spirit* was first poured out. He was given to set apart and give power to believers for Christ's mission of bringing the gospel to the world. This event is seen by most theologians to be the beginning of the church. (See also Holy Spirit; Passover.)

PENTECOSTALISM. A term used to describe a movement in the church that began in 1901. It emphasizes the use of all the spiritual gifts, especially the miraculous*

* Defined elsewhere in Dictionary

ones. It also teaches that the baptism with the Holy Spirit*
comes after conversion* which is power for serving God
and others. Speaking in tongues* (using a language that
the speaker does not know) is the evidence of that
baptism. They usually form new Pentecostal churches. In
this way it is different from charismatics* who usually try
to renew and reform the churches they are in. (See also
Baptism In/With/Of The Holy Spirit; Charismatic
Movement; Spiritual Gifts; Tongues, Speaking In.)

PERFECTIONISM. The Wesleyan* teaching that a
person can become completely holy* in this life. We are
made holy by grace* through faith, not by works. It is
often defined as "perfect love." Some even say it means
never to sin.* It is also called entire sanctification* or
"second blessing."* Most other theologies do not believe
it can happen in this life. (See also Entire Sanctification;
Good Works; Holy, Holiness; Sanctification; Second
Blessing; Wesleyan.)

PERICHORESIS. (From Greek: perichoresis, two parts
living in each other.) Two things living in, and deeply
affecting each other. It refers to the three persons in the
Trinity* being a part of each other. It also is used to
describe the relationship between Christ's human and
divine* natures. (See also Communication of Attributes,
Communicatio Idiomatum; Hypostatic Union; Trinity.)

PERSEVERANCE. The teaching that believers must
keep on being faithful to God. They must continue
believing in Jesus to the end of their lives. They might
backslide.* However, if they are true believers, they will

always return to their faith. According to Calvinists,* it is the other side of a belief in eternal security* (God will keep secure those whom he has chosen for salvation). It is the "P" in Calvinism's TULIP.* (See also Assurance; Backsliding; Eternal Security; TULIP.)

PERSON. Used technically to refer to the Trinity* and God.* (1) In the Trinity it refers to the three selfs in God's being. (2) It is a part of who God is. He can think, feel and decide, which is part of being a person. (See also God; Trinity.)

PERVASIVE DEPRAVITY. (SEE TOTAL DEPRAVITY.)

PHARISEES. (1) An important Jewish* religious group that was strong during the time of Jesus. They tried very hard to follow the Jewish laws. Jesus often criticized them for following the small details of the law, but not loving God or other people. They were the main enemies of Jesus. (2) Today people are called "Pharisees" who try to be very good on their own without God's help. They often judge other people. They are self-righteous* and hypocrites.* (See also Hypocrisy; Judaism; Sadducees.)

PHILOSOPHY. (From Greek: philos, love, and sophia, wisdom, knowledge.) The way a person or system looks at the whole of life and the world. It studies such areas as what is real (metaphysics*), how we know truth (epistemology*) and what we should do (ethics*). (See also Epistemology; Ethics; Metaphysics.)

PIETISM. (From Latin: pietas, devotion, religion.) A type of Christianity that focuses on living a holy* life. It has four main characteristics. (1) Personal experience is very important. (2) The Bible is its focus. (3) It is very serious about living a holy* life. (4) It tries to work against the spiritual deadness in the churches of the day. (See also Holy, Holiness; Renewal.)

PLENARY INSPIRATION. (From Latin: plenus, full.) All of the Bible* is inspired.* The whole Bible is the Word of God,* not just parts of it. (See also Inspiration, Bible; Verbal Inspiration.)

PNEUMATOLOGY. (From Greek: pneuma, spirit and logos, word.) It is the part of theology* that deals with the Holy Spirit.* It includes both who he is and what he does. (See also Baptism In/Of/With the Holy Spirit; Holy Spirit.)

POLITY. (SEE CHURCH GOVERNMENT.)

POLYTHEISM. (From Greek: poly, many, and theos, God.) The belief in many gods. It is a part of many Eastern and African religions. (See also Animism; Monotheism; Spiritism; Theism.)

POPE. (From Greek: papas, father.) The office of the bishop* of Rome, the earthly leader of the Roman Catholic* Church. The pope is the person who fills that office. He is believed to be in the direct line from Peter (Matt. 16:18 19). (See also Apostolic Succession; Catholicism, Roman.)

POSTMILLENNIALISM. (From Latin: post-, behind, after, mille, thousand, and annus, year.) The view that the time of peace and righteousness* will be started by the preaching of the gospel* by the church. There will be so many people converted that, by the power of the Holy Spirit, the rule of Christ will begin. Jesus will rule spiritually through Christians. His second coming* will be after this time of peace. There are several types of postmillennial views. (See also Amillennialism; Eschatology; Millennium; Premillennialism; Second Coming of Christ.)

POSTRIBULATION. (From Latin: post, after.) One of the views about the rapture,* the time God will take the church out of the world. It is the view that the church will go through the whole tribulation* (a time of great trouble at the end of the age*). God will protect them during that time. After that they will be taken up out of the world to be with Christ. This view is usually connected with premillennialism* (Christ will come before his 1000 year rule) or amillennialism* (now is the time of Christ's rule). (See also Amillennialism; Eschatology; Great Tribulation; Midtribulation; Premillennialism; Pretribulation; Rapture; Tribulation.)

POURING. One form of baptism.* Water is poured over the person's head. This form of baptism pictures the Holy Spirit being poured out on God's people (Acts 2:17). It is often called "Effusion." (See also Baptism; Immersion; Sprinkling.)

POWERS. Spiritual forces at work in the world. They

are usually evil. Christ created them (Col. 1:16), but now they work against him. The main places Paul uses the term are Rom. 8:38; Eph. 1:21; 6:12; Col. 2:15. Some believe they are angelic beings (demons*). Others believe they are the structures of society. (See also Demons, Demon Possession.)

PRACTICAL THEOLOGY. A term that is used for the relating of theology* to the practice of ministry.* It includes areas like worship,* preaching, and Christian education. (See also Pastoral Theology; Systematic Theology.)

PRAISE. Joyfully announcing how great God is. It is declaring the wonder of God. It is thanking him for whom he is. The OT teaches that it is done most correctly out loud when believers are gathered together. However, it is proper at any time, in any way and with any number. (See also Hallelujah; Hosanna; Joy.)

PRAYER. Speaking to God. It can include praise,* thanks, telling God about our sin (confession*), or asking for something for ourselves or another. We can come to God only through Christ and only because he invites us. (See also Intercession; Lord's Prayer.)

PREDESTINATION. (From Latin: praedestinare, foreordain.) (1) In general, God's decision before the creation* of the world about everything that would happen. (2) Specifically, in salvation* it refers to God's choice of certain people to be saved. It is understood in two ways: God chooses just those who will be saved (election*); or God chooses both those who will be saved and lost (reprobation*). Also, the basis for predestination is understood in different ways. Arminian-ism* says God knows ahead of time who will believe and chooses them (foreknowledge*). Reformed Theology* says God chooses based on his decision alone and then those people believe (effectual calling*). (See also Decree; Double Predestination; Elect; Election; Preterition; Reprobation; Salvation.)

PRE-EXISTENCE OF CHRIST. The belief that Christ was the Second Person of the Trinity* before he became human. He was God before he became the man Jesus. He has always been and will always be God. (See also Christology; Deity of Christ; Incarnation.)

PRE-EXISTENCE OF SOULS. A teaching about the beginning of each person's soul.* It says that souls are alive with God before they are put into human bodies at birth. It is mostly a non Christian view. Mor-monism teaches pre-existence of souls. Two opposite views are Tradu-cianism* (soul comes from parents) and Creationism* (God makes each new soul when he puts it in a body). (See also Creationism; Soul; Traducianism.)

PREMILLENNIALISM. (From Latin: prae-, before, mille, thousand, and annus, year.) The view that the millennium* will be set up when Christ returns at the end of the age. His coming will be sudden (imminent*). He will establish his rule as Messiah* over the whole earth. It will be a time of righteousness* and justice.* The view is often tied with a literal* understanding of OT prophecy*

and a restoration of Israel. (See also Amillennialism; Eschatology; Literalism; Millennium; Postmillennialism; Second Coming of Christ.)

PRESBYTERIAN GOVERNMENT. (From Greek: presbyteros, elder.) A way that some churches are organized. Authority* is given to the leaders whom the church chooses to represent them. Those leaders are called elders or presbyters. Its model is the Jerusalem Council in Acts 15. There are higher groups of elected representatives called presbyteries (local), synods (regional), and the General Assembly (entire church). (See also Authority; Church Government; Congregationalism; Episcopal Government.)

PRESERVATION. The teaching that God keeps alive that which he created.* He sustains it (Col. 1:16 17). It is a part of God's providence* (his care for his creation). It is also called "conservation." (See also Providence.)

PRETERITION. (From Latin: praeter, to pass over.) The teaching that God "passes over" those whom he does not choose for salvation.* He lets them go their own way and die for their sin.* He does not actively choose some people to send to hell. This is in contrast with election* in which he does actively choose some people to save. Preterition focuses on human choice. Unbelievers are responsible for their choice to reject God. It is a part of some forms of Calvinism.* (See also Double Predestination; Predestination; Reprobation.)

PRETRIBULATION. (From Latin: prae-, before.) One

of the views about the rapture,* the time God will take the church out of the world. The view that Christ will take the church out before the time of great suffering at the end of the age* (the tribulation*). After that, he will return with the church to set up his kingdom.* It includes the belief that Jesus can return at any minute to take the church (imminence*). (See also Eschatology; Great Tribulation; Imminence; Midtribulation; Postribulation; Rapture; Tribulation.)

PREVENIENT GRACE. (From Latin: prae-, before, and venire, to come.) Literally, "the grace that comes first," before human decisions. It is the Wesleyan* and Arminian* teaching about God's grace.* (1) Wesleyans say it is the grace given to all people before salvation.* No one can respond to God's grace because of sin.* But then God gives all people this grace, making them able to believe. They may either accept or reject salvation. (2) Arminians and others use it for "common grace,"* the grace God gives in keeping all creation* alive, limiting sin, etc. (See also Arminianism; Irresistible Grace; Wesleyan.)

PRIDE. The attitude of thinking of yourself more highly than you really are. Looking down on other people is usually a part of it. God says he hates pride (Prov. 6:17). We are to be humble* instead. (See also Humility.)

PRIEST. A person who represents humans in God's presence. It is used in many ways. (1) In the OT, a priest offered sacrifices* for people and prayed* for them. (2) In the NT, Jesus is our High Priest* (Heb. 7 9). He offered himself as our sacrifice and is now in heaven praying for us. (3) In the NT also, all believers are to be priests for each other (1 Pet. 2:9). (4) In some churches today, a priest is the leader of the church who represents the people before God. (See also High Priest; Intercession; Offices of Christ; Sacrifice.)

PRIESTHOOD OF ALL BELIEVERS. The NT teaching that all Christians can come into God's presence (1 Pet. 2:5). We do not need anyone to stand between God and us. Christ did that by his death on the cross. We also can pray for others like a priest* did. It is a Protestant* teaching. (See also Mediation, Mediator; Priest.)

PROBLEM OF EVIL. (SEE THEODICY.)

PROCESS THEOLOGY. A system of theology* that became popular in the 1960's. It was started by the theology of Charles Hartshorne (1897-) and the philosophy of Alfred North Whitehead (1861-1947). It teaches that everything is changing and growing. God is so much a part of the world that he is changing and growing also. (See also Panentheism.)

PROCESSION OF THE SPIRIT. (SEE FILIOQUE.)

PROGRESSIVE REVELATION. The teaching that God revealed himself over a period of time. Revelation* gradually got fuller by stages. The later revelation builds on the revelation that was already given. The later revelation includes new truth* as well as truth that is more complete. But that new truth does not contradict the older truth. Therefore, the older truth looked forward to the revelation of Christ (Lk. 24:44; Heb. 1:1-2.) (See also Hermeneutics; Revelation.)

PROGRESSIVE SANCTIFICATION. A view of how a Christian becomes holy.* It teaches that we grow to be holy over a period of time. Only in heaven* will we be completely holy. It does not happen in an instant. (See also Perfectionism; Sanctification.)

PROLEGOMENA. (From Greek: pro, before, and lego, to speak.) Literally, the words spoken before. It is the topics that must be covered before getting to the theology* itself. It includes topics like how to do theology (method) and what theology is (nature). In some theologies it includes the study of revelation.* (See also Revelation; Systematic Theology; Theology.)

PROMISE. A statement to another person that you will or will not do something in the future. The Bible teaches that God made many promises to his people. It also teaches that he is faithful and does what he promises. The main promise that the OT looked forward to was a Savior,* Jesus. (See also Covenant.)

PROPHET, PROPHECY. A prophet is a person who speaks for God to the people. A prophecy is the message itself. There were many prophets in both the OT and NT. The Bible teaches Jesus is the greatest prophet. A prophet has two jobs: (1) forthtelling, giving God's message to the people, and (2) foretelling, announcing what will happen in the future. Prophecy is also listed as one of the spiritual gifts* (1 Cor. 12:10). People disagree about whether God still gives prophecies today. (See also Offices of Christ; Promise; Spiritual Gifts.)

PROPITIATION. (From Latin: pro-, before, and petere, to seek.) The turning away of anger by an offering. In theology it is the idea that Christ died to take away God's anger (wrath*) toward human sin.* Some people disagree because saying God is angry seems to make Him not perfect. The NT speaks of propitiation in Rom. 3:25; Heb. 2:17; and I Jn. 2:2; 4:14. (See also Atonement; Expiation; Salvation; Wrath.)

PROTESTANTISM. The group of Christian churches which separated from the Roman Catholic* Church (the church connected with the Pope*) in the 16th century. They disagreed with or "protested" some of the teachings and practices. The main teaching of Protestantism is the central authority of the Bible.* It is also distinct from Roman Catholicism in other ways. (1) God alone is to be given glory,* not any humans, saints,* or the church.* (2) Humans are saved* by God's grace through faith alone, not by human actions. (3) All believers are priests to one another (priesthood of all believers*). (4) There are only two sacraments* or ordinances.* They are baptism* and the Lord's Supper.* It is all Christian churches which are not Roman Catholic or Eastern Orthodox.* (See also Catholicism, Roman; Orthodox Church.)

PROVIDENCE. The teaching that God takes care of his creation.* There are three aspects to providence. (1) He guides it to his purposes (divine government*). (2) He upholds it and keeps it alive (preservation*). (3) He uses the free actions of humans to carry out his purposes (con-cursus*). (See also Concursus; Government, Divine; Preservation.)

PURGATORY. (From Greek: purus, clean, pure, and agere, to do.) The Roman Catholic* teaching about a place between heaven* and hell.* They believe people go there who are going to heaven, but are not yet perfect. They are not evil enough to go to hell. It is a place of punish-ment that makes people pure enough to go to heaven. It burns off venial sin,* those which can be forgiven. People do not stay there forever, but just until they are holy enough. (See also Catholicism, Roman; Hell; Intermediate State; Judgment.)

PURIFY, PURIFICATION. To make clean, holy.* In the OT it is used to speak of both ritual cleanness and holiness of character. In the NT it is used to speak of the blood* of Christ making us clean from sin.* (See also Clean, Unclean; Salvation.)

QUMRAN. (SEE DEAD SEA SCROLLS.)

RANSOM. The process in which a slave or prisoner is freed by payment of a price. In the NT, Christ paid the price to free us from sin.* That price was his death. The Bible never says who receives the payment. (See also Atonement; Atonement, Ransom Theory; Redemption.)

RAPTURE. (From Latin: rapio, caught up.) The belief that Christ will take the church* out of the world to be with him at his second coming.* It is based on I Thess. 4:15 17. There is disagreement on whether it will happen before, during or after the great tribulation.* There is also disagreement on who will be taken. (See also Eschatology; Great Tribulation; Midtribulation; Postribulation; Pretribulation; Second Coming of Christ; Tribulation.)

RATIONALISM. (From Latin: ratio, reason.) An emphasis on reason. It is the view that everything that can be known is known by reason. It is often opposed to empiricism,* knowing things by our senses and ex-perience. In theology it is the belief that we can prove there is a God or know spiritual truths by our reason. (See also Empiricism; Epistemology; Philosophy.)

REAL PRESENCE. A view of the Lord's Supper.* It teaches that the body and blood of Christ are "in, with, and under" the bread and wine. It is based on Jesus' words, "this is my body." It is taught by Lutherans.* It is often called Consubstantiation. (See also Dynamic Presence; Lord's Supper; Lutheranism; Memorialism; Transubstantiation.)

REALIZED ESCHATOLOGY. The view of the end times of Charles Dodd (1884-1973), a British scholar, and others. It says the Kingdom of God* has already been fulfilled or "realized." It was started during the life of Jesus and is already here. There is no time in the future when God will fulfill the promises because he already has. (See also Eschatology; Inaugurated Eschatology.)

REBAPTISM. The act of baptizing* a person a second time. It is often done because the first baptism was when the person was an infant or baptism was done in a different form. (See also Baptism; Baptism, Infant.)

RECONCILIATION. (From Latin: re-, back, again, and conciliare, to bring together.) Making good the relationship between two people or groups again. Christ died on the cross to bring peace between God and humans. We had been friends with God before Adam sinned.* Then we were enemies after sin. We were reconciled, made friends again, when Christ died to take away the cause of hatred. (See also Atonement; Propitiation.)

RECONSTRUCTION THEOLOGY. (SEE THEONOMY.)

REDACTION CRITICISM. (SEE CRITICISM, REDACTION.)

REDEEMER. (From Latin: red-, back, and emere, to get, buy.) The one who pays the price to free a person from punishment. In the NT, Christ is the one who died to free us from the penalty of sin.* (See also Atonement; Deliverance, Deliverer; Redemption; Savior.)

REDEMPTION. (From Latin: red-, back, and emere, to get, buy.) Set free, rescued, delivered,* liberated from oppression. It is the means by which a person is saved.* The Exodus is the main OT example of redemption. Another OT example is the kinsman-redeemer (i.e., the book of Ruth) who rescued a widow from poverty by marrying her. In the NT, Christ died on the cross to pay the penalty for sin. It is related to ransom, the custom of paying a price to release a slave or prisoner. (See also Atonement; Messiah; Ransom; Savior.)

REFORMED TRADITION, THEOLOGY. A term used to speak of Calvinistic* theology as different from Lutheran* and other theologies. John Calvin (1509-64) of France and Ulrich Zwingli (1484-1531) of Switzerland were the first leaders. There are several teachings which make it distinct from Lutheranism, Wesleyanism, and other theologies which are not Reformed. (1) God is to be known as sovereign;* he rules over everything. (2) Humans cannot resist the grace of God (irresistible grace*). (3) They teach Covenant Theology.* (4) God makes believers holy gradually over time (progressive sanctification*). (5) The law* is to be used to guide a believer. Within these teachings, much difference in theology is allowed. It often includes a pres-byterian* form (representative) of church government.* (See also Calvinism; Presbyterian Government; Protestantism.)

REGENERATION. (From Latin: re-, again, back, and generare, to give birth, to produce.) The Holy Spirit's work of giving new spiritual life* to a person who believes in Jesus. A person's heart* was once dead because of sin. When a person believes, God makes that heart alive (Tit. 3:5). It is also called new birth or being born again* (Jn. 3:3). (See also Born Again; New Creation, New Creature; Salvation.)

REINCARNATION. (From Latin: re-, again, in, in, and

caro, flesh.) The non Christian belief that a soul passes through many different lives. After a person dies they live again in another body, or even an animal or plant. Their state in the next life is based on how good or bad they have been in this life. It is a part of Eastern religions and New Age teaching. (See also Death.)

REMISSION OF SINS. (SEE FORGIVENESS.)

RENEWAL. To make new or give new life. It is used for awakening or a deepening spiritual life* that has become dull (Rom. 12:2; Eph. 4:23). It can refer to either persons or churches. (See also Regeneration.)

REPENTANCE. To be sorry for doing wrong and turn away from it. It means to turn away from sin* and turn toward God. It is a part of conversion.* It also happens throughout a Christian's life when sin is discovered. (See also Conversion; Penance; Salvation.)

REPROBATION. (From Latin: reprobare, to reprove, punish.) It is the Calvinistic* teaching about God's relationship to those he did not choose to save. There are two views. (1) Most often it means that God decided to pass over those not chosen and let them die in their sins.* This is "soft Calvinism." This is also called preterition.* (2) Sometimes reprobation is understood as God choosing some people to send to hell. It is "stronger Calvinism." It is the negative side of double predestina-tion.* (See also Calvinism; Double Predestination; Elect; Election; Predestination; Preterition.)

RESTRAINER. The one who holds back the power of lawlessness in 2 Thess. 2:7. In the last days* this one will be "taken away," no longer will stop the evil. The restrainer is usually understood as either the Holy Spirit* or the church.* (See also Last Day(s).)

RESURRECTION. The bringing back to life after one died. It is used in two different ways. (1) It usually refers to when Christ came back to life on the third day. (2) It also refers to the raising of the bodies of believers and, in some theologies, unbelievers. This will happen at the end of the age.* (See also Crucifixion; Eschatology; Resurrection, First; Resurrection of Christ, Resurrection of Christ, Resurrection of the Dead, Bodily; Resurrection, Second.)

RESURRECTION, FIRST. A phrase in Rev. 20:5 which is understood in many ways. Amillennialists* (who believe the rule of Christ is now) usually see it as a spiritual raising. They see it happening to believers either at conversion* or after death when they will rule with Christ. Premillennialists* (who believe Christ will return before his 1000 year rule on earth) see it as the bodily raising of believers at the end of the age.* (See also Resurrection, Second.)

RESURRECTION OF CHRIST. The fact that Jesus died and rose from the dead on the third day. He came back into the same body, though it was now glorified. The whole Christian message is based on this truth. That is why in the Bible it is often used to refer to the gospel* as a whole (Acts 4:2; Rom. 1:4). (See also Crucifixion;

Resurrection.)

RESURRECTION OF THE DEAD, BODILY. The teaching of the Bible that God will raise all the dead to life in the future. They will be given new bodies. Those bodies will be united with their souls. We can know this is true because Christ was raised again (I Cor. 15). There are many views on when this will happen and the type of bodies. (See also Eschatology, Resurrection.)

RESURRECTION, SECOND. An idea taken from Rev. 20:1 6 which speaks of the "first resurrection."* Many people say this suggests there must be a second. It is the resurrection right before the Great White Throne judgment. Many amillennialists* (who believe the rule of Christ is now) see it as bodily raising of all who have died. Premillennialists* (who believe Christ will return before his 1000 year rule on earth) see it as the bodily raising of unbelievers. They see it as involving those who are not raised until after the 1000 year rule of Christ. (See also Resurrection, First.)

REVELATION. (From Latin: revelare, to draw back the veil or curtain.) That which was made known which was hidden before. In theology it refers to God telling us that which we could not know without Him. It often refers to the Bible.* (See also Bible; Bibliology; Revelation, General; Revelation, Special.)

REVELATION, GENERAL. The part of what God has shown us about himself that all people can see. It comes through creation,* what humans are like, etc. It shows us that there is a God, his power, his goodness, etc. However, it does not tell us how to be saved* (as special revelation* does). All who reject it are judged guilty.* There is debate on the result of general revelation. It is sometimes called Natural Revelation. (See also Natural Theology; Revelation; Revelation, Special.)

REVELATION, NATURAL. (SEE REVELATION, GENERAL.)

REVELATION, SPECIAL. What God has shown us that tells people how they can be saved.* The Bible* and Jesus* are the two main types of special revelation. It includes both God's actions and his words. (See also Bible; Jesus; Revelation; Revelation, General.)

REWARDS. Something given as a payment for an action done. In theology, it is most often used to refer to what God will give believers in the future for the good they have done. 1 Cor. 3:9 15 and 9:16 27 are the main passages that teach about rewards. (See also Eschatology.)

RIGHTEOUSNESS. Doing and thinking what is good, holy,* right and pure. It is used in many ways. (1) God is perfectly righteous. His law* is perfect and he does what is pure, right and good. (2) God makes believers righteous (justification*). He transfers the righteous standing of Christ to all believers (Rom. 5:15). We are no longer guilty.* (3) Believers are commanded to live righteously. We are to act and think in the pure way God does. God helps believers become righteous in their character (sanctification*). (See also Attribute of God; Holy,

Holiness; Justification, Justify; Original Righteousness; Sanctification.)

RIGHTEOUSNESS, ORIGINAL. (SEE ORIGINAL RIGHTEOUSNESS.)

ROMAN CATHOLIC. (SEE CATHOLIC, ROMAN.)

RULE OF FAITH. A summary of the truths of the gospel* which Christians are expected to believe. The term was first used in the second century. Today, Protestants* call the Bible* "the only rule of faith and practice." Roman Catholics say "rule of faith" is the whole teachings of the church. (See also Creed; Orthodox, Orthodoxy.)

SABELLIANISM. (SEE MONARCHIANISM.)

SACRAMENT. (From Latin: sacramentum, a thing set apart as holy.) A religious action or ceremony that was given a special meaning by Jesus. It is a sign or means of God's grace* given to the people who are part of the sacrament. In most Protestant* churches it refers to baptism* and the Lord's Supper.* The Roman Catholic* Church has seven sacraments. Because the Catholic Church saw them having almost magical power, many evangelical* churches now use the term ordinance.* (See also Baptism; Ex Opere Operato; Lord's Supper; Means of Grace; Ordinance.)

SACRIFICE. (From Latin: sacrare, holy, and facere, to make.) The offering of something for the sake of someone else. (1) It is most often used for the purpose of atonement,* becoming right with God. (2) It is also used to praise,* worship,* or thank God. (3) In the OT an animal, food from the field, or another special object was the sacrifice. (4) In the NT, Christ is the one who took away our sin.* (5) Believers are also called to offer their bodies as "living sacrifices" (Rom. 12:1). (See also Atonement; Priest.)

SADDUCEES. An important Jewish* religious group that was strong during the time of Jesus. They believed only the first five books of the OT was the Word of God.* They also did not believe in angels* or resurrection.* They were the theological liberals* of their day. They opposed Jesus' ministry. (See also Judaism; Pharisees.)

SAINT. (From Latin: sanctus, holy.) Holy* person; someone who is set apart for God. (1) In the NT, all believers are called saints. (2) In the Roman Catholic* Church it is a title for those who were especially holy. Catholics believe they are now in heaven* with God praying* for people. (See also Canonization; Holy, Holiness.)

SALVATION-HISTORY. (SEE HEILSGESCHICHTE.)

SALVATION. (From Latin: salvus, safe.) God rescuing humans from sin* and bringing them into relationship with himself. Christ's death is the basis of salvation. In theology, it is often used for just the point at which a person enters into relationship with God (conversion*, justification*). But the Bible also uses it for the continual process of being made holy* (sanctification*) and the future time of being in God's presence (glorification*). (See also Atonement; Savior.)

SANCTIFICATION, PROGRESSIVE. (SEE PROGRESSIVE SANCTIFICATION.)

SANCTIFICATION. (From Latin: sanctus, holy.) To be made like God, holy.* At salvation* we are made holy in our position before God. Sanctification is also making us holy in our moral character. There are many questions about how this happens. Does it happen all at once or over a period of time? How holy can we become (i.e., without sin)? Who does the work   God or humans? (See also Holy, Holiness; Glorification; Justification, Justify; Perfectionism; Progressive Sanctification; Salvation.)

SATAN. (From Hebrew: Satan, enemy.) A name for the devil meaning the enemy or the one who stands against (God and believers). He is a high ranking spirit-being (angel*) who was created by God. He rebelled against God and was sent out of heaven.* He is the leader of all the demons* and everything that is opposed to God. He tries to get belie-vers to do evil and tries to hurt them. God will throw him and his followers into the lake of fire* at the end of the ages.* (See also Adversary; Demons, Demon Possession; Lake of Fire; Occult, Occultism.)

SATISFACTION. (From Latin: satis, enough, and facere, to make.) Payment of a debt that is owed. It is usually used to speak of the Satisfaction theory* about Christ's death. (See also Atonement; Atonement,

Satisfaction Theory; Propitiation; Sacrifice.)

SAVIOR. (From Latin: salvus, safe.) The one who saves, rescues or delivers.* (1) In the OT, God is the one who physically rescued his people both from their enemies and from evil. It also looked forward to the Messiah,* the one who would completely deliver* God's people and bless* them. (2) In the NT, Jesus is called the only Savior (Acts 4:12). He is the promised Messiah who would save his people. By his death he saves people from sin* and its effects. (See also Deliverance, Deliverer; Jesus; Messiah; Redeemer; Salvation.)

SCAPEGOAT. One of the goats used on the Day of Atonement* (Lev. 16). All the sins of the people of Israel were symbolically* put on the goat. Then the goat was sent off into the wilderness and never seen again. This was to show God's complete forgiveness* of their sins.* (See also Day of Atonement; Forgiveness.)

SCHISM. (From Greek: schisma, division, split.) A division or split of the church.* It is a group that separates from the unity* of the church. It is different from a heresy* because it does not necessarily teach wrong beliefs. It just divides from the church. (See also Cult; Heresy; Sect; Unity.)

SCRIPTURE. (SEE BIBLE.)

SECOND ADVENT. (SEE SECOND COMING OF CHRIST.)

SECOND BLESSING. The teaching that there is a second major work of God after a person is saved.* (1) It is a certain point in time when God makes a person holy* (entire sanctification*). The person is made "perfect in love." It is a part of Wesleyan* theologies. (2) Sometimes it refers to baptism in the Spirit.* (See also Entire Sanctification; Second Work of Grace; Baptism In/Of/With the Spirit.)

SECOND CHANCE. The belief that an unsaved person will have another chance after death to believe in Christ. This view is not taught in the Bible (Lk. 16:19 31; Heb. 9:27). (See also Universalism.)

SECOND COMING OF CHRIST. The belief that Christ will come to earth again. Jesus came to earth the first time as a baby and died on the cross. Then he was raised from the dead and later went up (ascended*) from earth into heaven* to go to be with his Father. But he will return bodily and it will be with power. Then he will judge* all people and will bring all things to their final purpose. (See also Advent; Epiphany; Eschatology; Imminent; Judgment; Marriage Feast/Supper of the Lamb; Millennium; Parousia; Rapture; Tribulation.)

SECOND DEATH. (SEE DEATH, SECOND.)

SECOND WORK OF GRACE. The teaching that there is a second major work of God after a person is saved. It is part of when God makes a person holy.* (1) It is used in Wesleyan* theology to speak of a second blessing* when God purifies* the heart. (2) It is also used with

Pentecostal* theology to speak of the baptism in the Spirit.* (See also Baptism In/Of/With the Holy Spirit; Second Blessing.)

SECT. (From Latin: sequi, to follow.) A group of people who have separated themselves from the church.* They teach truths which are different from the Bible or what is commonly believed by Christians (heresy*). They have their own beliefs and practices. "Sect" is usually used for cults* after they have grown larger and are more accepted. Often a strong leader is the center of it. Sometimes it is called a cult. (See also Cult; Heresy; Schism.)

SECULARISM. (From Latin: saeculum, age, long period of time.) A way of life or thought that is without God or religion. It is living life as if there is no God. It says religion should only affect the private and not public areas of life. This world is the focus of life, not God. It is some-times called "practical atheism."* It is often combined with some type of humanism* (valuing humans most highly). (See also Anthropocentrism; Atheism; Humanism; Secular Humanism.)

SECULAR HUMANISM. (From Latin: saeculum, age, long period of time.) The belief or practice that since there is no God (atheism*), humans are the highest of all beings. They are to be highly valued. They are the focus of all of life. The Bible speaks of this sinful attitude in Rom. 1:25. (See also Anthropocentric; Atheism; Humanism.)

SECURITY OF THE BELIEVER. (SEE ETERNAL

SECURITY.)

SELF-RIGHTEOUS. A term to describe people who believe they are good and accepted by God because of their own standards. They try to make themselves good by their own works apart from God. They do not usually trust in Christ's death on the cross. (See also Good Works; Pharisees.)

SEMI PELAGIANISM. (From Latin: semi, partly.) A theology that began in the fifth century that rejects both Pelagianism* and Augustinianism.* Their main teaching is that humans work together with God in salvation (synergism*). They say God did not choose people whom he would save before the world began (predestination*). Instead, people believe based on their own free choice. (See also Augustinianism; Pelagianism; Synergism.)

SENSUS PLENIOR. (From Latin: sensus plenior, fuller meaning.) It is a principle of interpreting the Bible. It is based on the belief that some passages have a "fuller meaning" than even the authors would have understood. It assumes what the OT authors wrote contains more meaning than they understood. The NT authors bring out this meaning. It is different from allegory in that only the inspired authors can bring out the fuller meaning. An example is when Hosea spoke of God calling his son out of Egypt (Hos. 11:1). However, Hosea was probably not aware Matthew would use the verse to speak of bringing Jesus back from Egypt (Matt. 2:15). (See also Heilsgeschichte; Hermeneutics; Inspiration, Bible.)

SEPTUAGINT. (From Greek: septa, seventy.) The oldest and most important Greek translation of the Hebrew OT. It is dated about the second century B.C. The abbreviation is LXX, the Roman numeral for seventy. That is because some say there were seventy (or seventy two) Jewish translators.

SERAPH, SERAPHIM. (SEE ANGELS.)

SHEKINAH. (Hebrew word: shekina, dwelling [of God's presence].) A term used for God's glory* which can be seen. It speaks of God's closeness with his people. It is usually used for the cloud that guided Israel in the wilderness (Exod. 40:36 38). (See also Glory; Tabernacle; Temple.)

SHEOL. (SEE HADES, SHEOL.)

SIGN, SIGNS. (SEE MIRACLES.)

SIN. An act or thought that is against what God wants us to do or think. It includes both what we do and what we fail to do. It also includes who we are. The main word used for sin means "missing the goal or mark." It separates us from God. The Bible says everyone has sinned (Rom. 3:10, 23). There are many different understandings of the nature of sin. Wesleyans* teach that sin is anything we choose to do against the known law of God. Calvinists* teach that sin is any coming short of God's glory, whether or not we choose to, or know it is sin (Rom. 3:23). Other words for sin are iniquity, trespass, transgression, unrighteousness and wickedness. (See also

Alienation; Confess, Confession; Forgiveness; Original Sin; Sin, Mortal; Sin, Venial; Unpardonable Sin.)

SIN, MORTAL. A sin which leads to spiritual death.* In Roman Catholic* theology, it is a sin which kills spiritual life.* The person knows the action is wrong and still intends to do it. If people die with mortal sin they have not confessed, they will go to hell.* Mortal sins are in contrast with "venial sins"* which are less serious. (See also Hell; Sin, Venial.)

SIN, VENIAL. (From Latin: venia, kindness, forgiveness.) A sin which can be forgiven.* In Roman Catholic* theology, it is a sin which weakens spiritual life,* but does not kill it. The person chooses to do the act, but does not intend to do wrong. If people die with venial sins they have not confessed, they will go to purgatory,* but not to hell.* Venial sins are in contrast with "mortal sins"* which are more serious. (See also Purgatory; Sin, Mortal.)

SINLESS PERFECTION. (SEE PERFECTIONISM.)

SOCIAL GOSPEL. (1) Specifically, a movement within theological liberalism* from about 1880 to 1929. It taught that the main responsibility of the church was to work to solve social problems. That was done especially by working for social justice* and changing social structures. They believed this was the way to bring the Kingdom of God.* (2) It is used generally for the Christian response to human need throughout the ages. (See also Just, Justice; Kingdom of God; Liberalism, Theological.)

SOCINIANISM. A theology started by Socinus (1539-1604) of Italy that had many errors. Its most important teaching is that Jesus died just to be a good example, not to take away the penalty for sin.* It also teaches that there are not three persons in the one God (Trinity*). Also, it teaches Jesus was not God until after he was raised from the dead. It became the theological basis for Unitarianism.* (See also Atonement, Moral Influence Theory; Christology; Deity of Christ; Trinity; Unitarianism.)

SON OF GOD. A title that spoke of a special relationship with God. It is used in the OT of kings, angels,* and Israel. In the NT, it is especially used of Jesus.* It shows that Jesus was God in a way that no one else was. It also is closely tied with the idea that Jesus was the Messiah,* the one looked forward to in the OT who would save his people. (See also Christology; Jesus; Messiah; Son of Man.)

SON OF MAN. A title that Jesus* often used to speak of himself. Dan. 7:13 is the main OT background for this title. It is a way Jesus claimed to be the Messiah,* the one sent from God who would save his people. (See also Christology; Jesus; Messiah; Son of God.)

SOTERIOLOGY. (From Greek: soteria, salvation and logos, word.) The part of theology* that deals with salvation.* It includes topics like how God calls people (calling*), rescues them from sin (salvation), and brings them into relationship (adoption*, union with God*). It also includes how he helps them grow in the Christian life (sanctification*), and what the goal is (glorification*). (See also Salvation; Systematic Theology.)

SOUL. (1) In the Bible, it is the person as created by God. It is the living being, the whole person. (2) In theology, it is used for the inner person, the part that is not physical. (See also Creationism; Dichotomy; Pre-Existence of Souls; Spirit; Traducianism; Trichotomy.)

SOUL SLEEP. A view of the intermediate state* (the time between death and when they are raised). It is the belief that the soul of a person sleeps during that time. This view is held by Seventh Day Adventists today. (See also Intermediate State; Soul.)

SOVEREIGNTY. Being in control of everything. God is sovereign. He has power over and rules everything. (See also Decree; Kingdom of God, Christ, Heaven.)

SPECIAL REVELATION. (SEE REVELATION, SPECIAL.)

SPIRIT. Literally, breath or wind. It can be used in two ways. (1) Often it refers to the Holy Spirit,* the third person of the Trinity.* (2) It is also the person in fellowship with God. Trichotomists* distinguish spirit from soul. The spirit is the part of the person which relates to God. (See also Dichotomy; Holy Spirit; Soul; Trichotomy.)

SPIRIT, HOLY. (SEE HOLY SPIRIT.)

SPIRITISM. The religion and practice of trying to contact dead people. This is usually done through a medium (a person whom they believe communicates between the earthly and spiritual worlds). The Bible clearly teaches spiritism is evil (Deut. 18:10 11; Rev. 22:15). (See also Demons, Demon Possession; Occult, Occultism.)

SPIRITUAL GIFTS. Gifts the Holy Spirit* gives to each believer. They are special abilities which are different with each person. They are given to build up the church. There are lists of gifts in Rom. 12:6 8; 1 Cor. 12:4 11; Eph. 4:11; and 1 Pet. 4:11. (See also Charismatic Movement; Miracles; Pentecostalism; Tongues, Speaking In.)

SPIRITUAL INABILITY. (SEE TOTAL INABILITY.)

SPIRITUAL LIFE. The life God gives a person when they are saved.* It is the openness to life beyond this world. It also refers to a person's own continuing relationship with God. (See also Regeneration.)

SPIRITUALITY. Being in close relationship to God. It is also being like God in character. It is the quality or nature of our relationship with God. (See also Imitation of Christ; Mysticism; Sanctification.)

SPRINKLING. One form of baptism.* Water is sprinkled on the person's head. There are two bases for this form. (1) "Sprinkle" is used in Ezek. 36:25 with the idea of making clean.* (2) It is much easier to do than putting the believer completely under the water (immersion*). Since it is often done by those who baptize infants, this becomes important. Because the NT does not give an exact form for baptism, the form must not be important. (See also Baptism, Infant; Immersion; Pouring.)

STEWARDSHIP. The careful use of the gifts God has given. It most often refers to money, but also to time, energy, other possessions, the earth, etc. It should be done by individuals as well as churches and larger groups. It comes from the belief that God made humans responsible to care for his creation (Gen. 1 3). (See also Tithe, Tithing.)

SUBORDINATIONISM. (From Latin: sub, under, below, and ordinare, to order.) A view of the Trinity* that says either Christ or the Holy Spirit is less important than the others, especially God the Father. Many people have taught this view, but it is not taught in the Bible. (See also Arianism; Monarchianism.)

SUBSTITUTION. (From Latin: substituere, to put instead of.) A person or thing that takes the place of another. It is especially used of Jesus' death in our place. (See also Atonement, Substitution Theory.)

SUPERNATURAL. (From Latin: super, above, and natus, born.) The belief that there is reality beyond or above the world we experience with our senses. It believes that there is a God,* angels* and demons,* life after death, etc. The Bible teaches that there is a supernatural world. The opposite is naturalism.* (See also Naturalism.)

SUPRALAPSARIANISM. (From Latin: supra, above, before, and lapsus, fall.) A Calvinistic* view of the logical order of God's decrees.* It refers to the order of the plan of God before the world began, not the order of events in history. It says that God decided to choose some for salvation* before he decided to let humans fall into sin.* The order of decrees is: (1) to choose some people to be saved and leave others in their sin; (2) to create those chosen people; (3) to let them fall into sin; (4) to send Christ to save those chosen for salvation. The opposite view is infralapsarian.* (See also Decree; Infralapsarian.)

SYMBOL. (From Greek: symbolon, to make a comparison.) A physical object that has come to stand for, point to, or represent something else. They may be related, but are not exactly the same. It is a sign of another thing. The Bible often uses symbols to explain truth.* For example, Rev. 1:20 uses seven candlesticks to stand for seven churches. (See also Hermeneutics.)

SYNAGOGUE. (From Greek: synagoge, a bringing together, assembly.) The Jewish* house of worship* and prayer.* There were many synagogues throughout Israel, but only one temple.* The reading of the OT was central in the synagogue service. It was different from the temple because there were no sacrifices* or priestly* services in the synagogue. Also, teaching was not done in the temple. There is disagreement about how synagogues began. Most people believe they began during the time the Jews were in

Babylon. (See also Judaism; Tabernacle; Temple.)

SYNCRETISM. (From Greek: synkretizein, to combine.) The combination of two or more different religions or beliefs so they form a new one. It is used to describe times in history when Christians combined the gospel with another religion or other beliefs. The result is that some central teachings are changed.

SYNERGISM. (From Greek: syn, together, and ergo, to work.) The view that God and man work together in some part of salvation. It is usually taught in the areas of conversion* or sanctification.* It is a way of explaining (1) God is in control, and (2) humans are responsible. (See also Monergism; Semi-Pelagianism.)

SYNOPTIC PROBLEM. (From Greek: syn, together, and optic, to see.) It is the question of why the first three gospels in the NT (Matthew, Mark, and Luke) are like each other in many ways, but very different in other ways. Many of the ideas and even the words are the same in all three. Sometimes they tell the same story, but the detail are merely different. Other times they seem to contradict each other. How did that happen? How they were written? Did they copy from each other? Did they all use a common source? There are many suggested answers to the questions. (See also Criticism, Redaction.)

SYSTEMATIC THEOLOGY. (From Greek: syn, together, and histanai, to set.) The logical, orderly study of the teachings of the Bible.* It involves several different steps. (1) It organizes the biblical teachings around certain topics (i.e., Christology,* Soteriology*). (2) It explores the relationship between these topics. (3) Then, it applies them to current issues and other areas of study. (4) It explains it in a way people can understand today. (5) Finally, some would include the defense of the teachings (apologetics*). Dogmatic* theology is another name for it. (See also Biblical Theology; Dogmatics.)

TABERNACLE. The tent which could be moved from place to place where the Jews* worshipped* God. It was made while they were in the wilderness during the Exodus. They used it until Solomon built his temple.* (See also Judaism; Temple.)

TELEOLOGICAL ARGUMENT. (From Greek: telos, end, or purpose.) The attempt to prove there is a God* because of the order in the world. Since there is order, purpose and design in the world, there must be an intelligent designer. Therefore, there must be a God. Sometimes this is called the Design Argument. (See also Cosmological Argument; Theistic Proofs.)

TEMPLE. (1) A building where God is worshipped.* In the OT, Solomon built the first temple. It was permanent and was much bigger than a tabernacle.* It was the place to offer sacrifices.* The temple was always in Jerusalem. The last one was destroyed in 70 A.D. and has not been rebuilt since. It was the place where God's was present. (2) Believers and the church are also called temples (2 Cor. 6:16; Eph. 2:21). In this sense, it is the place where God is present, worshipped and made visible. (See also Holy of Holies; Tabernacle.)

TEMPTATION. It has two different meanings. (1) It is trying to get a person to do wrong. Satan does this. God never tempts a person to sin (Jas. 1:13). (2) It also means testing a person to show their spiritual strength. God does this (Job 1; Gen. 22). (See also Satan; Sin.)

TESTAMENT. (1) Originally, a covenant* or promise.* (2) It is the name given to the two major parts of the Bible the OT and the NT. (See also Bible; Covenant.)

TESTIMONY. (SEE WITNESS, TESTIMONY.)

TETRAGRAMMATON. (From Greek: tetra, four, and gramma, a letter.) The four Hebrew letters (YHWH) for the personal name of Israel's God, Yahweh.* (See also Yahweh.)

TEXTUAL CRITICISM. (SEE CRITICISM, TEXTUAL.)

THEISM. (From Greek: theos, God.) The belief in God.* It usually means belief in one God (monotheism*). It also usually means a personal God who is involved in his creation* (as opposed to deism,* an impersonal God). (See also Agnosticism; Atheism; Deism; God; Theistic Proofs.)

THEISTIC EVOLUTION. (From Greek: theos, God.) The view that God created the world by using evolution.* It teaches that he started every-thing. In the beginning he created a simple living thing. Over time it changed into a very complex human being. It tries to combine the truth

---

of both the Bible and science. (See also Creation; Evolution.)

THEISTIC PROOFS. (From Greek: theos, God.) The attempts to prove there is a God.* These arguments are often divided into ones based on reason and experience. It is done without special revelation,* the Bible. (See also Anthropological Arguments; Cosmological Argument; Moral Argument; Ontological Argument; Teleological Argument.)

THEOCENTRIC. (From Greek: theos, God, and kentrikos, center.) The belief or practice that God* is the center of everything. God and his purposes are most important, not humans or anything else. (See also Anthropocentric.)

THEOCRACY. (From Greek: theos, God, and kratein, to rule.) The rule of God. A form of government which is under the law* of God. God planned for Israel to be a theocracy. (See also Law; Sovereignty; Theo-nomy.)

THEODICY. (From Greek: theos, God, and dike, justice.) A way of trying to solve "the problem of evil." It tries to show that God is just* and good in his relationships with people. It tries to give an answer to three truths which seem to contradict each other. The three truths are: (1) God is good and (2) all powerful, (3) yet evil things happen. (See also Evil; Omnipotence.)

THEOLOGY. (From Greek: theos, God and logos, word.) (1) In a broad sense, the study God's relationship with persons. (2) In a narrow sense, it is the study of God* alone (Theology Proper*). (See also God; Systematic Theology; Theology Proper.)

THEOLOGY PROPER. (From Greek: theos, God and logos, word.) The part of theology* that deals with God. It includes topics like what God is like, the Trinity,* how we know Him, and his work. (See also Creation; Decree; Election; God; Providence; Trinity.)

THEONOMY. (From Greek: theos, God, and nomos, law.) Literally, God's law.* It is a movement to make everyone follow the OT (Mosaic) Law.* It is also called Dominion or Reconstruction Theology. (See also Law; Mosaic Law.)

THEOPHANY. (From Greek: theos, God and phainein, to appear.) A time when God let humans see or hear him. It includes events like the burning bush to Moses (Exod. 3:2 6) and the still small voice to Elijah (1 Ki. 19). (See also Anthropomorphism.)

THEOTOKOS. (Greek word: theotokos, mother of God.) A title for Mary, the mother of Jesus. In 431 A.D. at the Council of Ephesus, it was used to claim that Jesus was God from before his birth. Now, it is used either to claim that Jesus is God* or to honor Mary very highly. (See also Catholicism, Roman; Deity of Christ; Pre-Existence of Christ; Virgin Birth.)

TITHE, TITHING. The practice of giving one tenth of one's income to God. It comes from the OT practice. It is not commanded in the NT. However, generous giving is strongly encouraged (1 Cor. 16; 2 Cor. 8 9). (See also Stewardship.)

TONGUES, SPEAKING IN. One of the gifts of the Spirit.* It means speaking to God in a language that the speaker does not know. NT examples are Acts 2; 1 Cor. 14. There is disagreement over whether they are earthly or heavenly languages. Tongues are important today in most Pentecostal* and charismatic* churches. (See also Charismatic Movement; Pentecostalism; Spiritual Gifts.)

TORAH. (SEE PENTATEUCH.)

TOTAL DEPRAVITY. The teaching that every part of humans is affected by sin.* Humans can do nothing to earn God's favor. This is a result of original sin,* the effect of Adam's first sin on all humans. It does not mean that humans are as evil as they could possibly be. It is also sometimes called Pervasive Depravity. It is part of Calvinism* and is the "T" in TULIP.* (See also Original Sin; Sin; Total Inability; TULIP.)

TOTAL INABILITY. The teaching that there is nothing a person can do to earn salvation* or God's favor (Eph. 2:8-9). Some people use the term "spiritual inability." (See also Good Works; Total Depravity.)

TRADITION. A group of teachings, practices or beliefs which are passed down from one generation to another. (See also Orthodox Church.)

TRADUCIANISM. (From Latin: traducere, to lead along.) A teaching about the beginning of each person's soul.* It says that a person's soul comes from their parents, just like their body does. It comes from the view that persons are a whole unit. It is one of the ways of explaining the belief that every person is born a sinner.* Two opposite views are Creationism* (God makes each new soul when he puts it in a body) and Pre-existence of souls* (souls are alive before being put into bodies). (See also Creationism; Pre-existence of Souls; Soul.)

TRANSCENDENCE. (From Latin: trans, over, and scandere, to climb.) The belief that God is separate and distinct from his creation.* He is also far above and much greater than it. God is not only in one place. This is often contrasted with the truth that God is immanent,* present with his creation and his people. (See also Attributes of God; Im-manence.)

TRANSFIGURATION. (From Latin: trans, over, and figura, to form, to shape.) The time when Jesus was on the mountain and his physical appearance was changed. His face glowed and his clothes became white as light (Matt. 17:2; Mk. 9:2 3).

TRANSGRESSION. (SEE SIN.)

TRANSUBSTANTIATION. (From Latin: trans, over, and substantia, to be present.) A view of the Lord's Supper.* It teaches that the bread and wine are changed into the body and blood of Christ. It is based on Jesus' words, "this is my body." It is taught by Roman

Catholics.* (See also Catholicism, Roman; Dynamic Presence; Lord's Supper; Memorialism; Real Presence.)

TRESPASS. (SEE SIN.)

TRIBULATION. The trouble and suffering of God's people. Often it is used for the great tribulation.* That is a time at the end of the ages* when there will be more suffering than any other time. God's purpose will be to judge* and purify.* People have many different views about how long it will be; some say seven years and others say just a period of time. There are also different views about how it fits with other end time events. (See also Eschatology; Great Tribulation; Midtribulation; Pretribulation; Postribulation.)

TRICHOTOMY. (From Greek: tricha, in three parts, and temnein, cut.) Dividing something into three parts. In theology, it is used for the view that humans are made up of three parts: body, soul* and spirit.* (See also Dichotomy; Soul; Spirit.)

TRINITY. (From Latin: trinus, three.) The belief in one God in three persons. God the Father, Jesus Christ* and the Holy Spirit* are equally God and share the same attributes.* They have all always been God. They are also three distinct persons.* Matt. 28:19 and 2 Cor. 13:14 are two places where all three are mentioned. It is also taught throughout the NT. (See also Christology; Pneumatology; Theology Proper.)

TRINITY, FIRST PERSON OF THE. God the Father.

(See also Theology Proper.)

TRINITY, SECOND PERSON OF THE. Jesus Christ,*
God the Son. (See also Christology.)

TRINITY, THIRD PERSON OF THE. The Holy
Spirit,* God the Spirit. (See also Pneumatology.)

TRITHEISM. (From Greek: tri, three, and theos, God.)
The belief that God* is three separate gods. It is a view of
the Trinity* that is not taught in the Bible. It does not
keep the unity* of God. (See also Monotheism; Trinity.)

TRUTH. That which agrees with reality. In a basic
sense, it is what agrees with the mind of God. It is used in
many ways. (1) It is one of the qualities (attributes*) of
God. 1 Sam. 15:29 teaches that God never lies.
Therefore, we can depend on him. (2) Jesus is the truth
because he shows the Father (Jn. 14:6). (3) In theology,
the Bible* is called the truth. (4) Also, believers are
commanded to live and tell the truth (Col. 3:9). (See also
Attributes of God.)

TULIP. An acrostic in which each letter represents the
first letter of a main points of Calvinism's* view of
salvation.* They are Total Depravity,* Unconditional
Election,* Limited Atonement,* Irresistible Grace,* and
Perseverance* of the Saints. All five letters are always
capitalized. (See Atonement, Limited; Calvinism;
Election; Irresistible Grace; Perseverance; Total
Depravity.)

TYPE. (From Greek: typos, form, pattern.) An event, person, ritual or institution (i.e., the priesthood) that was a pattern of someone or something in the future. The type is the earlier event; the antitype is the later event. The type helps us understand the later antitype. It is espe-cially used of something in the OT that represents something of greater importance in the NT. Most often they point to Christ. An example is the flood and baptism* (I Pet. 3:21). Another example is Adam and Christ (Rom. 5:14). A type differs from an analogy* in that both the type and antitype were historical. (See also Hermeneutics; Typology.)

TYPOLOGY. (From Greek: typos, form, pattern and logos, word.) A method of interpreting the Bible that tries to understand types.* It studies OT events and persons to find the importance for similar NT events and persons. This study must follow what the Bible says about how the events are the same, rather than imagined similarities. (See also Hermeneutics; Type.)

UNBELIEF. A lack of faith.* Usually it refers to not believing in God or the Christian faith. It can be choosing to reject God, a lack of faith, or just doubt. It is often seen as the basis for all sin.* (See also Agnosticism; Atheism; Sin.)

UBIQUITY. (SEE OMNIPRESENT.)

UNCLEAN. (SEE CLEAN.)

UNCTION. (SEE ANOINT.)

UNION WITH CHRIST. The part of salvation* in which a believer becomes united with Christ. Christ's death and resurrection* become a part of our experience. We also share in his life and righteousness. (See also Identification with Christ; Justification, Justify.)

UNITARIANISM. (From Latin: unus, one.) (1) The belief that teaches that God is only one person.* Therefore, Jesus* and the Holy Spirit* are not God. They deny the biblical teaching of Trinity* (three persons in one God). (2) It is also the name of an organized religious group that teaches this. This group also believes in Universalism.* (See also Arianism; Monotheism; Trinity; Universalism.)

UNITY. To be one. (1) It is used mostly to talk about the church. There is only one church, the body of Christ. Eph. 4:4 6; Gal. 3:28 and other passages clearly teach this. (2) It is also used to speak of the oneness of the Father, Son and Holy Spirit in the Trinity.* (3) Also, believers are united with God. (See also Church; Ecumenical, Ecumenism; Trinity; Union with Christ.)

UNIVERSALISM. (From Latin: universus, all together.) (1) The belief that in time all people will be brought into relationship with God. All people will be saved.* They will all be restored to God eventually. The Bible does not teach this view. (2) It is sometimes used for the truth that the gospel* is for all people. It is not limited to only a certain group of people. The Bible does teach that the gospel is for all (Matt. 28:19; Acts 10-11). (See also Second Chance; Unitarianism.)

UNLIMITED ATONEMENT. (SEE ATONEMENT, UNLIMITED.)

UNPARDONABLE SIN. The sin that cannot be forgiven.* Jesus says it is "blasphemy* against the Holy Spirit" in Mk. 3:28 29. There are many different understandings of this verse. Most often it is seen as a con-stant unbelief* or denial of the work of God. (See also Blasphemy; Sin; Sin, Mortal.)

UNRIGHTEOUSNESS. (SEE SIN.)

VENIAL SIN. (SEE SIN, VENIAL.)

VERBAL INSPIRATION. The belief that the very words of the Bible are inspired.* The Holy Spirit moved the authors to use certain words and not just certain ideas. (See also Inspiration, Bible; Plenary Inspiration.)

VICARIOUS ATONEMENT. (SEE ATONEMENT, VICARIOUS.)

VIRGIN BIRTH. The teaching that Mary, Jesus' mother, had no sexual relations with a man before he was born. Jesus was conceived by the power of the Holy Spirit. (See also Christology.)

VISIBLE CHURCH. (SEE CHURCH, VISIBLE.)

WESLEYAN. A system of theology* started by John Wesley (1703-91) of England. It is a part of the Protestant* tradition. Three main beliefs make it different from Reformed theologies.* (1) Prevenient grace* is the teaching that God gives all people the ability to believe. (2) Un-limited atonement* is the belief that Christ died for all, not just the elect.* (3) Entire sanctification* or perfectionism* is the teaching that a believer may become completely holy* in this life. (See also Arminianism; Calvinism; Protestantism; Reformed Tradition, Theology.)

WHOLLY OTHER. A term used to speak of God being totally separate from his creation.* He is unique, different from everything else. It is sometimes used like "transcendence."* It is used by neo-orthodoxy* to deny immanence* (God is present in this world). It was in response to the theological liberals* who said God is only in the hearts of people. (See also Neo-Orthodoxy; Transcendence.)

WICKED, WICKEDNESS. (SEE SIN.)

WILL OF GOD. What God wants to happen. Often it is spoken of in different ways. (1) God's "decretive* will" decides everything that will happen and is hidden. (2) God's "preceptive will" is what he tells us to do, his moral law.* (3) God's "permissive will" is what he lets happen even if it is not what he wants to happen. (4) Sometimes "will of God" is used for God's plan for an individual's life. (See also Decree; Freedom, Free Will, Freedom of the Will; Providence; Sovereignty.)

WISDOM. Generally, it means being skilled, being able to make a plan to get the right results. In the Bible, it means living life under God's direction. Used in many ways. (1) It is one of God's attributes.* In this sense it is that God knows everything that is good and does the good (Ps. 104:24). (2) It is a good quality that those who love God are to seek. It comes from fearing (respecting) the Lord (Prov. 1:7). (3) It is a type of literature in the Bible. It includes the books of Job, Proverbs, and Ecclesiastes and parts of other books. (4) It is one of the spiritual gifts* given to believers (1 Cor. 12:8). In this sense it is an ability to decide between good and evil. (5) It is represented as a woman in Proverbs 8. Some people understand this to be Christ, the Second Person of the Trinity.* (See also Attributes of God; Spiritual Gifts.)

WITNESS, TESTIMONY. To tell others what you have seen or experi-enced. It is especially used of telling others about Jesus or the gospel.* All believers are called to be witnesses (Acts 1:8). (See also Evangelism.)

WORD, WORD OF GOD, WORD OF THE LORD. Three terms used for God speaking his message to human. In the OT, these terms are used to show that the message comes from God. In the NT, "Word" or "Word of God" can mean either the OT (Jn. 10:35) or Jesus (Jn. 1:1 4; Logos*). Today it is used to speak of the Bible or Jesus. (See also Bible; Logos; Revelation.)

WORK OF CHRIST. The part of theology* that deals with Christ's ministry.* It is especially what he did while he was on earth. It focuses on what he did on the cross to save humans (atonement*). It also includes his present ministry of praying for believers. (See also Atonement; Intercession.)

WORK, WORKS. Acts that are done to accomplish something. Believers are commanded to do the work of God. But we can never earn God's favor or salvation. This is called "salvation* by works." The Bible teaches strongly against this. (See also Good Works.)

WORLD VIEW. The way of looking at life. It includes the things we assume about the world. It includes what we believe about God,* the world,* life, sin,* death,* history, etc. It affects how we see and inter-pret all of life. (See also Culture.)

WORLD, WORLDLINESS. (1) It often means the earth as different from the heavens. (2) It also can mean all people. (3) In the NT it also has the evil meaning of Satan's* system which is opposed to God. (4) Worldliness is always used in the evil sense of liking that which is evil and opposed to God. (See also Evil; Satan; Sin.)

WORSHIP. To give honor to God; to declare worthy. It is giving him the special honor that he alone deserves. People can worship by praising* God and praying* to him. They also can worship by serving him. The Bible says true worship is done in love, truth, respect and humility.* (See also Church; Praise; Prayer.)

WRATH OF GOD. That part of God's character which opposes, hates, and punishes sin.* Some say God does not have wrath. That would make God evil. But both the OT and NT say much about God's wrath. His anger at sin is different from ours. It comes from his holiness* and not selfish emotion. Therefore, God's anger is not evil. The

Bible teaches that Jesus' death took away God's wrath toward humans because of sin (1 Jn. 2:1-2). (See also Judgment; Propitiation.)

YAHWEH. (Hebrew word from: hwh, to be.) The personal name for the God of Israel. It had special meaning because God gave it at the same time as he remembered his covenant* with Abraham, Isaac, and Jacob (Exod. 3:14-15). People disagree on its meaning. The two ways it is most often translated are "I am who I am" or "I will be what I will be." The Jews* did not want to say God's name because of the third commandment (Exod. 20:7). So they used Adonai* (Lord) or "The Name." Later others came up with the name, "Jehovah." It is a Germanized combination of the consonants from Yahweh and the vowels from Adonai.* It is not a biblical word at all. (See also Adonai; Tetragrammaton.)

Made in the USA
Columbia, SC
07 January 2019